From the Roof of the World:

Refugees of Tibet

From the Roof of the World:

Refugees of Tibet

Dharma Publishing

From the Roof of the World:
Refugees of Tibet

All proceeds from the sale of this book
will be used to preserve the Tibetan heritage.

This publication is sponsored by a grant from
the Barr and June Rosenberg Foundation.

ISBN: 0-89800-241-9

The photograph on the cover was taken in the spring of 1959, in the earliest days of the exodus from Tibet.

Photographic credits: cover photo and pages 67–81, 83–113 courtesy of Marilyn Silverstone/Magnum Photo Agency; pages 82, 270, 274 courtesy of Howard Davidson; page 269, courtesy of Cynthia Dean; page 20, courtesy of John Gage; pages 4, 40, 43, courtesy of the Library, The Academy of Natural Sciences of Philadelphia; pages 154, 258, 260 courtesy of Mark Richmond; pages 2, 5, 37, 45, 46 by Joseph F. Rock © National Geographic Society; pages 123, 126, 127, 168 courtesy of Linda Schaeffer; pages 272, 273, 275 courtesy of Claire Thompson

Editing and design by Dharma Publishing
Typeset in Mergenthaler Palatino
Printed and bound in the USA by Dharma Press

00 99 98 97 96 95 94 93 92 9 8 7 6 5 4 3 2 1

Contents

Dedicated to the people of Tibet

Publisher's Preface

In the late 1960's, over 100,000 Tibetan refugees were living in settlement camps in India, Sikkim, Nepal, and Bhutan. At that time, the Tibetan Aid Project (TAP) began operation out of a small office in Berkeley, California.

TAP was founded by Tarthang Tulku, a Tibetan lama who had come to America in 1968. Its purpose was to send financial aid directly to the Tibetan refugees. TAP set up a penfriend program that connected Western sponsors to Tibetans in need of support. All work was done by volunteers, and every penny donated to TAP was used to benefit the refugees and to coordinate the various activities. Administrative expenses were kept to a bare minimum.

Through the penfriend program, hundreds of Americans sent $10–15 a month directly to Tibetan penfriends. Even this small contribution made a significant difference in the lives of the refugees: It could save a family from going hungry, send a child to school, help a monk to study and practice, or provide essential medical care.

Reorganized under the umbrella of the Tibetan Nyingma Relief Foundation in 1974, TAP has worked with the Tibetan Nyingma Meditation Center (TNMC) to support Tibetan refugees in a number of ways: through the penfriend program, by sponsoring ceremonies, through sending Dharma books and thanka reproductions to the refugee monasteries, and by sponsoring visits by lamas to the United States. Although TAP is in the Nyingma tradition, it seeks the preservation of all forms of Tibetan Buddhism, and has given support to all the schools and sects.

Over the past twenty-two years TNMC and TAP have collected many photographs from Tibetan refugees. Some came from the individuals and groups TAP sponsored: Each refugee requesting a penfriend sent his or her photo to TAP, and groups performing ceremonies also sent photographs at TNMC's and TAP's request. Some Tibetans enclosed photographs in their letters to Tarthang Tulku simply because they wanted to share their accomplishments with him. Westerners who visited the refugee camps sometimes returned with photographs as well.

This material was not always kept in an organized way, but even though each person, group, or place can no longer be identified with complete accuracy, and the photographs are not organized year by year, they form a valuable record. On seeing these pictures, Tibetans who have lived through the experience of being refugees can remember the history of these difficult times. So that this record, incomplete though it is, would not be lost, TNMC and TAP asked Dharma Publishing to put these photographs together and publish them. This book, prepared by Dharma Publishing under their auspices, and with valuable guidance from Tarthang Tulku, is the result.

Looking back, those who have been involved with TAP over the years have considered its approach to supporting the Tibetan refugees and the preservation of Tibetan culture only partially successful. Although in some cases penfriends have become longterm friends able to support one other spiritually and personally, even exchanging visits, not all the penfriend relationships have been so mutually rewarding. This may have to do with different expectations and social patterns that prevent real communication. Western society is very mobile, and it is not unusual to change jobs and relationships every three to five years. Not realizing this, Tibetans

may not understand why their penfriend relationship does not last, or why letters do not come regularly. Westerners, for their part, may be interested in subjects their Tibetan penfriends do not readily discuss, and may tire of hearing about the more commonplace aspects of daily life. Language barriers also play a role.

Logistical difficulties have affected communication as well. Even when Western penfriends have sent contributions regularly, Tibetans have not always been able to depend on receiving mail. Lack of familiarity with Western banking procedures has sometimes made the routine act of check-cashing difficult. We have tried to smooth out some of these details by routing penfriend contributions through TAP to refugee monasteries, but this approach has also been subject to some of the same difficulties.

Perhaps there is a better way to support the Tibetan refugee communities on a broader scale. Since our organization is small and lacks major supporters and access to large funds, there is a limit to what we can do. But if supporters of the Tibetan refugees from all over the world would do as we have done, our combined efforts could make a substantial difference. This possibility is still open, and we welcome inquiries. Anyone interested in helping, or simply wanting to know more about TAP and its activities, should contact Dharma Publishing.

To supplement the record presented here, we have provided brief introductions to the history, land, and culture of Tibet. Many Westerners today have an interest in Tibet and its culture, but very few people have studied Tibetan history. Nor is it easy to do so. Some of the material available on the subject is incomplete or lacking in fair-mindedness; other material is written for specialists rather than general readers. Although in the near future we may be able to offer a fuller account of Tibetan history, in this volume we have presented a brief survey that can offer a basic orientation.

Familiarity with the story of Tibet is especially important for Tibetan refugees, many of whom may not know their own history well. Thus, the survey is intended to be particularly relevant to the Tibetan refugees themselves.

Similarly, the sections on land, Dharma, and culture are offered to the refugees to help them deepen their knowledge of their heritage, that they may understand more fully who they are, what Tibet is, and where Tibet and Tibetan culture stand at present.

It is Dharma Publishing's hope that this book will strengthen the faith and determination of the Tibetan refugees, reminding them of what has happened since 1959— what has been lost and what has been accomplished through their efforts in India and elsewhere. We offer this book in commemoration of all the Tibetan people who have died under tragic circumstances since 1959, in Tibet and abroad.

Foreword

After I came to America and opened the Tibetan Nyingma Meditation Center in 1969, my students and I did whatever we could to help the Tibetan refugees. We collected old clothes and shoes and sent them to India. At one point we even shipped tons of survival biscuits from Civil Defense bomb shelters in Los Angeles. Although this project presented a tremendous task of coordination and communication for our small group, the benefit to the refugees was less than we had hoped, because the food did not keep well in the Indian heat.

Other approaches were more successful: Through the penfriend program, hundreds of Americans were able to help Tibetan refugees in India, Nepal, and Bhutan. Encouraged by TAP and its activities, many Americans also gave direct aid independently. In 1974, when TAP was reorganized under the Tibetan Nyingma Relief Foundation, the penfriend program continued; today the program is active in Europe and

South America as well. Many people have also helped to support the new refugee monasteries.

Over the past twenty years, many Westerners have aided the Tibetan refugees through TAP and TNRF, and on behalf of the Tibetan refugees, being a Tibetan myself, I want to acknowledge and thank everyone who has given support. In particular, I appreciate very much the help Americans have given to my people and my country. Other organizations have done much more, but we have been able to make this small gesture because I have been here in this country, and because many American people have helped me.

My acknowledgement and thanks also go to the TNMC students who have worked for TAP, especially Judy Rasmussen, who has helped to administer TAP since the early years, and more recently, Victoria Riskin. Two of my students, Zara Wallace and Jack Petranker, prepared this book for publication at my request, and I appreciate very much the good job they have done. Leslie Bradburn also contributed in many valuable ways. I give special thanks to June and Barr Rosenberg, who made possible the publication of this book through their sponsorship.

Over the years, Tibetan refugees in India and Nepal have sent me many photographs of their activities, including ceremonies we have sponsored, and these photographs, combined with the snapshots Tibetans seeking penfriends have sent to TAP, provide the heart of the book. Many important centers and lamas have been left out, simply because we had no photo-graphs available. The photographs of the earliest days of the refugees in India were given to me by Marilyn Silverstone of the Magnum Photo Agency, to whom I am grateful.

Our primary purpose in publishing this book is to offer these images to the refugees themselves, that they may more fully understand and appreciate the value of the experiences recorded here. In keeping with the policies TAP and TNMC have followed since their earliest days, TAP will use all proceeds from the sale of the book to benefit the Tibetan refugees.

Tarthang Tulku
December, 1991

Refugees of Tibet

Mi-nyag Gangs-dkar with the cloud veil thrown back.

The Land of Tibet

In the highlands of Tibet, nature exerts a power that is matched in few places on earth. Usually bathed in sunshine, whose power creates the bluest lakes in the world, Tibet is truly a land where earth and sky meet in splendor.

The Tibetan plateau is the highest inhabited land anywhere on earth, with an average elevation of some 11,000 feet, the elevation of the capital city of lHa-sa. The area of the plateau is just slightly smaller in size than India, and four times the size of the state of Texas.

Despite its great height, the land of Tibet is not inhospitable, except in certain desert regions. Winters are cold, long, and difficult, but the sun shines almost daily, warming the heart. At lHa-sa, the temperature in summer can reach 85 degrees Fahrenheit, while the minimum in winter only drops to a few degrees below zero. Some of the nomads who make their homes as high as 17,000 feet above sea level seldom venture into the lower valleys for fear of the intense heat.

Nor is there a great deal of snow in Tibet. Except in some of the mountain ranges, about two to four feet a year is typical. Still, the land is challenging: Its vast open spaces and steep mountains make travel difficult, and have contributed to striking differences in culture, language, and history from valley to valley.

Because of its great size, Tibet varies widely in its geography. Recurring features are the high mountains that ring it on three sides, the vast stretches of steppes, suitable for grazing and a nomadic way of life, and the river valleys that allow for agriculture. Most of the far north is taken up by the Byang-thang, a vast desert with great salt lakes that supports few living things. In recent centuries, the far west, the region known as mNga'-ris, has also become in-

3

A short, steep pass leads from the 'Phan-po Valley into the lHun-grub Valley.

creasingly desert-like. To the southeast, the land descends down toward the ocean, becoming semi-tropical.

The Formation of the Plateau

Ancient Tibetan accounts agree with modern scientific findings in holding that Tibet at one time was a vast sea, out of which the great mountains that surround the plateau emerged. According to modern geology, the Himalayan mountain ranges were created when the tectonic plates on which Asia and the Indian subcontinent 'ride' collided some fifty million years ago, making this the youngest mountain range in the world. The land south of the gTsang-po river appears to belong to the tectonic plate that carries India, while the rest of Tibet rides on the Asian plate. The northern parts of Tibet are the oldest, and it appears that the land that forms the Tibetan plateau was added to Asia gradually, with the southernmost portion being the last to join.

For reasons that are not fully understood, the Himalayas began to rise quite rapidly some two million years, becoming the highest mountain range on earth. As they gained in height, they blocked out moist winds from the south, so that rainfall and snowfall decreased. As a result, the lakes of the Tibetan plateau shrank in size. Especially in the north, they often became salt lakes. In other areas, dense forest gave way to grasslands. The Himalayas continue to thrust upward today, at rates that are calculated to vary from between one to five inches a year.

4

The A-mnyes-rma-chen mountain range.

The continuing movement of the earth's crust on the plateau is evidenced by the intense geothermal activity, deep fault zones, and frequent severe earthquakes. Seven great earthquakes have rocked Tibet in this century, but only one took place in the interior of the plateau: a major tremor near lHa-sa in 1951. The vigorous changes still taking place on the plateau match the sense of the Tibetan people that theirs is a land of powerful forces and strong energies. The major mountains of Tibet have always been revered as homes of powerful spirits that guard the land.

Mountains and Rivers

Tibet stands unique among the world's lands in the extent of its mountain ranges. These mountains in turn give rise to eight of the world's great rivers, which flow through South Asia, shaping civilization all along their course. This interplay of mountains and river valleys has influenced most of Tibet, not only geographically, but culturally as well.

Especially in the east, the rivers have cut deep gorges through the land, creating a dramatic landscape that isolates different regions from one another. In central Tibet, the river valleys are broader, supporting agriculture and a more settled way of life.

The North The northern border of Tibet is marked by the Kun-lun mountain range (including the Kokoshili range). The longest moutain range in Asia, it separates the Byang-thang desert from the Tarim basin. The western portion of the Kun-luns is the highest, with many peaks over 20,000 feet in height; the highest mountain is Ulug Muztagh, at 25,476 feet. The mountains are mostly very weathered, and thus more dome-like in shape.

North and east of the Kun-luns are the Altyn Tagh and the Nan Shan mountain ranges. This is the site of the desert-like region of Tsaidam, the location for the large lake known as Koko Nor, which is more than sixty miles across.

The East gNyan-po gYu-rtse, a sacred mountain that rises 16,490 feet, lies in the Bayankara mountain range, sometimes considered an eastern extension of the Kun-luns. It formed about two hundred million years ago.

The Bayankaras are the source for three great rivers. The rMa-chu originates in the Bayankaras, then flows east through 'Gu-log, makes a huge turn called the knee, or khug-pa. It flows on through A-mdo and into China, where it is known as the Huang-ho or Yellow River (sixth longest in the world). The Nyag-chu is known in its upper reaches as the Dza-chu; later, as it enters into China, it is known as the Yalung.

Farther east and to the north lies the A-mnyes-rma-chen range, whose dominant mountain (20,610 feet in height) bears the same name. Famed as the home of the god rMa-chen-spom-ra, this peak, together with gNyan-po gYu-rtse, is considered a protector of 'Gu-log. Both are important pilgrimage sites. The story of the epic hero Gesar is connected to A-mnyes-rma-chen.

The lDang-la range parallels the Bayankara to the southwest, forming a natural barrier between Khams and dBus-gTsang. It is the source of the 'Bri-chu, which becomes the Yangtze river (fifth longest in the world), the rDza-chu, which eventually becomes Mekong river of Southeast Asia, and the Nag-chu, known in Southeast Asia as the Salween.

The province of Khams is often referred to as the land of Six Ranges and Four Rivers; it is rugged terrain known for its deep river gorges and steep slopes. Among the famous mountain ranges of Khams are Zab-mo-sgang, Mi-nyag-sgang, sMar-khams-sgang, Spo-bo-sgang, gYar-mo-sgang, and Tsha-ba-sgang.

Central and West The Transhimalaya mountain ranges (which include gNyan-chen-thang-la and Gangs-ti-se) divide the arid lands of the Byang-thang plain from the more fertile valleys of the south, where the gTsang-po river flows. The holy mountain of gNyan-chen-thang-la is 23,390 feet in height, while further west lies Mt. Kailaśa, one of the most sacred mountains of the world, which rises to a height of 22,156 feet.

Southwest of Kailaśa (known also as Ti-se) is the holy lake of Manasarowar. Nearby four of the great rivers of Asia originate: the gTsang-po, or rTa-mchog-kha-'bab (known in India as the Brahmaputra), the Glang-chen-kha-'bab (Sutlej), the rMa-bya-kha-'bab (the Karnali, which joins with the Ganges), and the Seng-ge-kha-'bab (Indus). Each is named for a particular animal that enjoys a special place in Indian mythology: the Horse, Elephant, Peacock, and Lion.

The South The Himalayas, which form the southern border of the Tibetan plateau, are the highest mountain range in the

Region of 'Gu-log, eastern Tibet.

world, with over 30 peaks more than
25,000 feet in height, including Mt. Everest,
Annapurna, Kanchenjunga, Kamet, Nanda
Devi, Gosainthan, Jomo Lhari, Phula Hari,
and Namchag Barwa.

The Regions of Tibet

Byang-thang and Tsaidam

The vast Byang-thang plain of northern
Tibet receives less than four inches of rain
a year; harsh and inhospitable, it is charac-
terized by strong winds, dust storms, and
extreme variations in temperature. The far
northwest is high cold desert while the
northern parts are rock-gravel desert, with

pockets of sparse, shrubby vegetation; in
the south there are areas of steppeland pas-
ture where a small number of nomads
make their homes. Only animals that can
adapt to the cold survive in Byang-thang;
these include the wild yak and wild ass,
the Tibetan antelope and gazelle, and the
blue sheep. Rivers flow from glaciers that
melt in summer, and salt lakes are abundant, with thick salt beds sculpted into unusual shapes by the high winds.

The Tsaidam region, a basin 46,000 miles
square, is similar in nature: arid and harsh,
with much of it true desert. It is rich in
natural resources such as coal and oil, tin,
copper, gold, and silver. The salt marshes

7

of Tsaidam shelter more than 200 species of birds.

A-mdo and 'Gu-log

A-mdo and 'Gu-log, in the northeast of Tibet, are generally dry, with steppe and meadowland on the mountain slopes; winters can be strikingly cold, with temperatures dropping as low as –36° F at A-mnyes-rma-chen and –16° F at Zi-ling.

These are lands of contrasts, with sharply defined seasons, grassy valleys set off by rugged peaks, and pockets of dense forest. In the steep, rocky gorges of the north is rich grassland and extensive glaciation on the mountain slopes. During the summer, the valleys are carpeted with small wildflowers that delight the eye and speak of nature's fantastic wealth. In the high, crisp mountain air, the breath is naturally light and calm, and the mind grows clear and sharp. The rivers run a deep, emerald green; in the winter they usually freeze to the bottom, and in the spring they melt slowly. The grasslands of the plateau provide excellent grazing for sheep, goats, horses, and especially yaks even as high as 18,000 feet, especially in the alpine meadows, where sedge and sagebrush can survive, despite permafrost.

'Gu-log, an area about 40,000 square miles in size (roughly the size of Greece), is bounded by the Bayankara mountains and the Oring and Tsaring lakes on the west. Its people are famed for their independence, and it seems that even in the times of the Mongol empire they never gave up their autonomy. Originally 'Gu-log was much larger, consisting of three large parts. The present region is only the area that had been called rMa-khog. A 'Gu-

log saying describes rMa as the poor mother who had seven strong sons.

Khams

The people of Khams have always been noted as fierce fighters. Large and imposing in appearance, strongly devoted in their loyalty, they were among the first to oppose the imposition of Chinese rule and also among the first to begin restoring temples and holy sites when the occasion arose in the past decade.

In the nineteeth century, Khams and especially sDe-dge (throughout most of Tibetan history, a separately ruled kingdom) served as the center of the important Ris-med movement, which sought to bring together the different Buddhist schools so that each could contribute its own heritage and knowledge for the sake of the Dharma.

In Khams and especially in southeastern Tibet, the tree line is higher, and much of the region is coniferous forest, though there are variations from one valley to the next. The far south, which drops in height below six thousand feet, is truly subtropical, affected by the monsoon winds from the Indian Ocean, and the wildlife there includes leopards and monkeys. Crops that will grow there include tea, grapes, coffee, bananas, and oranges, while native plants include laurel, rhododendron, laurel, azaleas, bamboo, and magnolia.

In the far southeast of Tibet, there are aboriginal hunters who use poisoned bows and arrows and in general follow a way of life usually associated with that of certain African tribes. This entire area is considered a powerful and sacred place.

Central and Western Tibet

The most important agricultural regions of Tibet are in the central area along the Yar-lung and gTsang-po rivers. Weather is mild and cool in the growing season, with many sunny days. In most parts of Tibet, agriculture is very limited, but here the crops available to be grown include wheat, barley, millet, and even rice, and in some areas apples, walnuts, and pears. Second harvests are even possible in some areas. High-altitude agriculture is possible because of the great amount of solar radiation absorbed by the plateau. This keeps the temperature higher than on steep mountainsides in other parts of the world.

The Yar-lung valley enjoys special fame as the birthplace of Tibetan civilization. The area known as gTsang runs west along the gTsang-po river, while dBus lies along the eastern course of the gTsang-po and along the sKyid-chu River to the north of the gTsang-po.

Western Tibet is sometimes known as mNga'-ris 'Khor-gsum (the three districts of mNga'-ris): Gu-ge, dMar-yul, and sPu-rang. Regions of alpine steppe are prominent along the south sides of the Gangs-ti-se Range, with many kinds of plants such as juniper, barberry, honeysuckle, and cotoneaster. In recent centuries, the area has been subjected to increasing desertification.

The fertile valleys, pastures, and forests that support the animals and inhabitants of the Tibetan plateau are closely tied to the whole Tibetan way of life. They have provided the raw material for its arts, sciences, and crafts, its medicine and art; while their beauty and power have inspired generations of Tibetans to draw closer to the forces of nature and the inner meaning of human life.

Yum-bu-bla-sgang, the castle built by the first king of Tibet in the third century B.C.

A Survey of Tibetan History

Tibetan history is a rich tapestry woven over more than twenty centuries. It is documented in the oral tradition, in written accounts that date back to the seventh century, and in records of other countries that had dealings with Tibet in this early era. Tibetan historians have composed comprehensive works on religious and political history. In addition, monastic histories, biographies, and lineage records have been carefully kept by the various schools and provide a fertile field for research.

An appreciation of the situation of Tibetan refugees requires at least some familiarity with the highlights of this history. In the West, very little has been known about Tibet until recent times, and so such knowledge is limited. In Tibet itself, very little emphasis was placed on the study of history. Today, with the fate of Tibetan culture still in the balance, it is important for Tibetans as well as Westerners to understand Tibet's historical development.

Tibet has a long and complex past. After the era of the Dharma kings, power shifted every century or so from one geographical region to another, and from clan to clan. The study of these changes reveals a delicate balance between worldly concerns and spiritual goals. There are deeds and facts that are difficult to reconcile with wise and compassionate leadership. Any civilization that endures for centuries, as Tibet's has, will have more and less enlightened eras. If we are to learn from history, it is important to shed light on the shadowy periods that are not now fully understood. Tibetan and Western historians have begun to study the facts presented in unbiased records and documents, and in time will be able to clarify the meaning of many events.

In this publication we offer our readers a brief outline of the major eras of Tibetan history. Our goal is to establish the context for the story of the Tibetan refugees and to encourage the further study of Tibetan history. Preservation of the rich civilization of Tibet depends not only on a concern for the future but also on an appreciation for the patterns of the past.

Archeological remains indicate that human beings were present on the Tibetan Plateau some 35,000 years ago. Farming villages date back to 3,500 B.C. and sites have been found at Chab-mdo in eastern Tibet and Nying-khri in central Tibet. The nomadic way of life likely developed after agriculture was established, judging from the evidence of other cultures.

Tibetan folklore speaks of the earliest inhabitants as mi-ma-yin, nonhumans of ten different kinds. They were magical, powerful, and mostly malignant in nature. At some point, human beings gained control of the land. The Maṇi bKa'-'bum describes how the first Tibetan people originated from the marriage of a female rock demon with a wise and compassionate monkey. The histories of the Tibetan tribes may eventually be traced in the accounts of the founding of different kingdoms, old family records, and the like. Some old records give a list of twelve important small kingdoms, while others give four cultures associated with early Tibet: 'A-zha, Zhang-zhung, Sum-pa, and Mi-nyag.

The history of the royal lineage is distinct from the history of the tribes. Most accounts agree that Yar-lung valley was the center of the early kingdom where the royal dynasty that began with gNya'-khri-btsan-po rose to power in the third century B.C. The earliest kings, known as the Seven Thrones, were magical beings who passed away leaving no trace. The eighth king, Gri-gum, was the first to die upon the earth. He was followed by the ninth king,

and then the Six Legs, the Eight lDe, and the Five bTsan. The last of these five, lHa-tho-tho-ri (b. 433 A.D.), was reigning when the Dharma first appeared in Tibet in the form of Buddhist texts and sacred objects. In a dream the king received a prediction that five generations later one would be born who could understand the significance of these things.

Four generations later, in the time of King gNam-ri, the Tibetan kingdom began to expand. His son, Srong-btsan-sgam-po, would found a true empire, while at the same time fulfilling the prophecy received by lHa-tho-tho-ri.

The first of the three great Dharma Kings, Srong-btsan-sgam-po is considered by the people of Tibet to be an emanation of Avalokiteśvara, the great Bodhisattva who has watched over and cared for the Tibetans since the time of the first human beings in Tibet. He resolved to take the major steps necessary to prepare the way for the coming of the Dharma.

During his reign Srong-btsan-sgam-po performed a series of actions any one of which would have made his reign notable. First he shifted the capital of Tibet from the Yar-lung valley to a new site on the sKyid river, north and west of the original capital. In later years it became known as lHa-sa.

The next step came when the king entrusted his minister, Thon-mi Sambhoṭa, with the all-important task of devising a suitable Tibetan alphabet, creating a grammar, and collecting and translating the first Buddhist texts. The king himself then composed the first major work in the new written language, the Maṇi bKa'-'bum, a history and spiritual guide for his people.

Through marriages to the Nepali princess Bhṛkuti (Khri-btsun) and the Chinese princess Kong-jo, both regarded as emanations of Tārā, Srong-btsan-sgam-po was able to secure precious Dharma blessings for Tibet. The two princesses brought with them two highly revered and powerful statues: the Jo-bo-chen-po, which was ultimately housed in the gTsug-lag-khang temple, and the Jo-bo-chung-ba, which found its home in the Ra-mo-che temple. In addition, the princesses were skilled in subjects vital to the transmission of the Dharma. Princess Kong-jo in particular helped Srong-btsan-sgam-po build temples in carefully chosen locations for the purpose of subduing the wild land of the Tibetan plateau.

Under the political and military guidance of Srong-btsan-sgam-po, Tibet became a powerful force throughout Asia, its sphere of influence reaching into China, Central Asia, Nepal, and even northern India. Through his charisma and conquests (said to have been accomplished more through the use of magic than by force) Srong-btsan-sgam-po was able to secure from India and other lands precious Buddhist relics and works of art.

The Dharma king also initiated a wide range of cultural contacts, inviting to Tibet many scholars, artists, and artisans. One well-documented instance is his invitation to physicians from India, China, and the Greek lands of the Byzantine empire. The latter, known as the 'Galen of Persia,' became the court physician.

Srong-btsan-sgam-po's grandson Mang-srong further expanded the Tibetan empire. During his reign conflicts with the

lHo-brag Khom-mthing   A 'border-subduing' temple founded by Srong-btsan-sgam-po.

Chinese empire of the T'ang dynasty became more frequent. Over the course of the next two centuries there were a series of clashes with T'ang China, and territory in Central Asia and western China often changed hands.

Early in the eighth century, Tibet forged alliances with the Turks and the Arabs and carried an offensive as far as Bru-sha (Gilgit). In 730, during the reign of Mes-ag-tshoms, a peace treaty between Tibet and T'ang China was signed, fixing firm borders between the two lands, but the fighting in Central Asia did not stop. Toward the end of Mes-ag-tshom's reign, Tibetan influence in neighboring regions expanded still further, reaching into Nan-chao (modern Yunnan) in the southeast.

Bang-so-dmar-po, the tomb of Srong-btsan-sgam-po, located near 'Phyong-rgyas in the Yar-lung valley, south of the gTsang-po.

14

In the second half of the eighth century, King Khri-srong-lde-btsan, considered an emanation of the Bodhisattva Mañjuśrī, invited to Tibet the Buddhist Mahāpaṇḍita Śāntarakṣita and the great tantric master Guru Padmasambhava. Working together, the king and the two great masters built the monastery of bSam-yas, Tibet's first center for the Dharma. Their action together is said to have been the result of a vow made jointly by the three leaders in a past life.

When bSam-yas was complete, the king officially proclaimed the Dharma the religion of Tibet and invited twelve monks from Kashmir to ordain the first Tibetan monks. He also invited Indian paṇḍitas to work with Tibetan lo-tsā-bas to translate thousands of texts into Tibetan, initiating one of the most comprehensive translation projects the world has ever known.

Khri-srong-lde-btsan continued to expand the Tibetan empire, making advances into China and regaining control over the ancient Silk Route through Central Asia. He concluded a short-lived peace treaty with T'ang China in 783.

Ral-pa-can, third of the great Dharma kings, came to power in about 817; honored as an incarnation of Vajrapāṇi, he gave his strong and active support to the Dharma. Among his accomplishments was instituting a program of revising and standardizing Buddhist translations. In 822, Ral-pa-can entered into a famous treaty that again fixed borders with T'ang China. Ral-pa-can's extensive support for the Sangha aroused the enmity of Bon ministers and nobility, who began looking for ways to seize power. In 836, Ral-pa-can

was assassinated, and his brother, Glang-dar-ma, seized the throne.

Before his own assassination in about 842, Glang-dar-ma instituted a policy of persecution toward the Dharma. Together with his other excesses, this attempt to destroy past accomplishments led to the loss of the empire, the fragmentation of the Tibetan kingdom, the suppression of the monastic Sangha, and a period of chaos and instability.

Glang-dar-ma's two sons, 'Od-srung and Yum-brtan, divided central Tibet between them, with Yum-brtan controlling the more easterly portion. His descendants continued to exert influence there. Although 'Od-srung's reign was marked by great disorders, he did not oppose the Dharma, and is even said to have constructed temples for the Sangha.

'Od-srung's son dPal-'khor continued his rule, but during the reign of dPal-'khor's sons, further disorders resulted in a new division of the kingdom. One of dPal-'khor's sons, bKra-shis-brtsegs, continued to rule in gTsang; in the next generation his sons founded the 'Lower Kingdoms' in Shangs, Nyang, and parts of the near west. dPal-'khor's second son, Khri-lde Nyi-ma-mgon, went to the far west, where his descendants later established the 'Upper Kingdoms', located in Gu-ge, Ladakh, and sPu-rang.

While these events were taking place in central and west Tibet, numerous kingdoms were forming in the east. Among them were sDe-dge and Gling (home of the famous ruler Ge-sar, who is said to have lived in the twelfth century). In the twelfth century 'Bru lHa-rgyal and his descen-

Rwa-sgrengs. Built by 'Brom-ston (1004–1064) north of lHa-sa in 1056, Rwa-sgrengs became the seat of bKa'-gdams-pa teachings and later a dGe-lugs-pa monastery.

dants founded the kingdom of 'Gu-log, situated between Khams and A-mdo.

With new texts becoming available and new teaching lineages being passed on, several schools were established at this time, including the bKa'-gdams-pa, the various branches of the bKa'-brgyud-pa, and the Sa-skya-pa. Together these schools were known as the gSar-ma or 'New' Schools; in contrast, the holders of the transmission that took place at the time of Padmasambhava became known as the rNying-ma-pa, or 'Ancient Ones'.

Early in the thirteenth century, Tibet's relations with the Mongols became vitally important in shaping its history. Under Chingghis Khan, the Mongols began to expand throughout Asia. By 1238 they had

seized China, Persia, and Russia, and threatened Europe. In 1244 Prince Godan, grandson of Chingghis Khan, invited Sa-skya Paṇḍita to visit the Mongol court. Arriving in Lan-chou in 1247, Sa-skya Paṇḍita established relations with the Mongols.

Godan's successor, Prince Qubilai, issued an invitation to the second Karmapa Karma Pakṣi and asked him to remain in his court, but the Karmapa left for Kara-korum to instruct the Great Khan Mongke, whom he converted to the Dharma. Qubilai also met with the siddha O-rgyan-pa, who offered him teachings.

In 1253 Sa-skya Paṇḍita's nephew 'Phags-pa (1235-1280) became the spiritual teacher of Prince Qubilai. When Qubilai rose to the rank of Great Khan in 1260, he installed

16

'Bri-gung-mthil. First founded northeast of lHa-sa by Mi-nyag-sgom-ring, it became the seat of 'Bri-gung sKyu-ra Rinpoche in 1179.

'Phags-pa as Ti-shih, a title given the Imperial Preceptor to the Emperor. Emperor Qubilai offered his teacher the territory of the thirteen myriarchies.

The Mongols also offered patronage to the Tshal-pa bKa'-brgyud and the 'Bri-gung bKa'-brgyud. When disputes between the Sa-skya and 'Bri-gung arose, Mongol chiefs took sides. The ensuing conflicts led to much loss of life in 1285 and again in 1290, when 'Bri-gung was burned. In 1332 the Third Karmapa, Rang-'byung-rdo-rje, and Toghon Temur, Mongol Emperor of China, met; in 1360 the Fourth Karmapa, Rol-pa'i-rdo-rje, also met with the Mongol Emperor.

This era was the time of Guru Chos-dbang, Rig-'dzin Kumārāja, dPang Lo-tsā-ba, gYung-ston-pa, Bu-ston Rin-chen-grub, and Kun-mkhyen Dol-bu-po.

By 1354 the influence of the myriarchy of Phag-mo-gru extended to most of dBus and gTsang. After a revolt in 1359 by 'Bri-gung came to an end, Byang-chub-rgyal-mtshan established a new system of administrative districts (rdzong-khag). Known as sDe-srid or T'ai Situ, Byang-chub-rgyal-mtshan was strongly influenced by the traditions of the ancient Dharma kings. He instituted laws based on the code of Srong-btsan-sgam-po.

This era was the time of Kun-mkhyen Klong-chen-pa, Rig-'dzin rGod-ldem, Bo-dong Phyogs-las-rnam-rgyal, 'Ba'-ra-ba-rgyal-mtshan, O-rgyan-gling-pa, rDo-rje-gling-pa, Re-mda'-ba, and rJe Tsong-kha-pa.

17

By 1436 the Rin-spungs princes in gTsang, former ministers of the Phag-mo-gru, were dominant in gShis-ka-rtse and by 1488 in rGyal-rtse. By 1498 their influence was felt in lHa-sa, where it lasted until 1517. Conflicts between Phag-mo-gru and the Rin-spungs-pa lords were intensified by their respective allegiance to the newly formed dGe-lugs-pa and the Karma bKa'-brgyud schools.

This was the era of Ratna-gling-pa, Rong-ston-chen-po, Ngor-chen kun-dga'-bzang-po, dGe-'dun-rgya-mtsho, mNga'-'ris Paṇ-chen, 'Bri-gung Rig-'dzin Phun-tshogs, dPa'-bo gTsug-lag-'phreng-ba, Rin-chen-phun-tshogs, Rig-'dzin Ngag-gi-dbang-po, Kun-mkhyen Padma dKar-po, and Sog-bzlog-pa.

In 1565 the gTsang-pa chief Tshe-brtan rDo-rje and his son bsTan-srung-dbang-po ended Rin-spungs-pa influence. By 1612 Phun-tshogs rnam-rgyal, Tshe-brtan's grandson, had control of gTsang. He and his son, bsTan-skyong dbang-po, later known as the sDe-pa gTsang-pa, entered dBus in 1618, gaining control of most of it.

When bSod-nams-rgya-mtsho, known later as the Third Dalai Lama, and Altan Khan, ruler of the Eastern Mongols, met in 1578, they established new relations between the Mongols and Tibetans. Mongol leaders again became involved in Tibetan affairs, supporting various factions and favoring one or another Buddhist school. Mongol armies were reported in central Tibet in 1607, 1610, 1618, and 1621.

This was the era of Jo-nang Kun-dga'-snying-po, lHa-btsun Nam-mkha'i-'jigs-med, Karmapa Chos-dbyings-rdo-rje, Rig-'dzin 'Ja'-tshon-snying-po, sTag-sham-nus-ldan-rdo-rje, and 'Brug-pa Ngag-dbang-rnam-rgyal.

In the 1630's Mongol tribes began arriving in the Lake Koko Nor region, led by Lingdan Khan, Chogthu Khan, and Gushri Khan, a Western Mongol prince of the Khoshot tribe. In 1635 Chogthu's son Arsalang led an army into Tibet. In 1639 Gushri Khan entered Khams, defeated the prince of Be-ri, and proceeded to central Tibet where he subdued the gTsang-pa princes in 1642. With Gushri Khan as his patron, the Fifth Dalai Lama (1617–1682) soon consolidated his leadership of Tibet, and his influence spread far and wide. He commanded the respect of both the Mongolian chiefs and Shun-chih, the second Manchu Emperor of China.

In 1679 the Fifth Dalai Lama appointed as sDe-srid (regent) the learned and astute Sangs-rgyas-rgya-mtsho, who made great contributions to Tibetan culture. With the passing of the 'Great Fifth', the sDe-srid conducted affairs for more than twenty years, but in 1705 lHa-bzang Khan, great grandson of Gushri Khan, entered central Tibet with his troops. The sDe-srid was betrayed and his regime destroyed.

This was the era of O-rgyan gter-bdag-gling-pa, sMin-gling Lo-chen Dharmaśrī, bDud-'dul-rdo-rje, Padma 'Phrin-las, Zhabs-dkar-tshogs-drug-rang-grol, Karmapa Ye-shes-rdo-rje, Paṇ-chen Chos-kyi-rgyal-mtshan, and Tshe-dbang-nor-bu.

lHa-bzang Khan was opposed by the Dzungar Mongol Tshe-dbang-rab-brtan (d. 1727), nephew of dGa'-ldan, the founder of the Dzungar Empire and son of Khung-Taiji. In 1717 Tshe-dbang-rab-brtan sent his brother Tshe-ring Don-grub with 6,000

dGa'-ldan monastery. Built in 1409 by Tsong-kha-pa near lHa-sa, dGa'-ldan was one of the major dGe-lugs-pa monastic universities. It housed 4,000 monks and had two major colleges.

troops to lHa-sa. Hundreds of monasteries were destroyed or damaged, especially those of the rNying-ma-pa school, and several major rNying-ma masters lost their lives.

By 1720, when Manchu troops of the K'ang-hsi emperor entered lHa-sa, Pho-lha-nas and Khang-chen-nas had expelled the Dzungars. Khang-chen-nas became first minister, and a four-man council was formed. Khang-chen-nas was killed in 1727, and Pho-lha-nas (Mi-dbang Pho-lha) rose to power. Following a brief reign by his son 'Gyur-med-rnam-rgyal, in 1751 the government was again reorganized, and in 1757 the office of rGyal-tshab (regent during minority of the Dalai Lama) was created.

The Eighth Dalai Lama was enthroned in 1762 and died in 1804; the Ninth lived only nine years, the Tenth to age nineteen, the Eleventh to age eighteen, and the Twelfth to age nineteen.

The Thirteenth Dalai Lama (1876–1933) presided over Tibet's entry into the modern international community of nations. With his passing in 1933, Rwa-sgrengs Rinpoche became regent, and soon proved a valuable leader. He located the Fourteenth Dalai Lama, bestowed his religious name, and ordained him. But political intrigue brought his career to an end, and he reportedly died in prison, though the full story remains to be told.

In 1950 the young Fourteenth Dalai Lama came to power, but in 1959 he had to leave the country. Since then Chinese Communists have controlled Tibet.

19

sTag-tshang Guru Padmasambhava practiced at the site of this monastery in Bhutan.

The Transmission of the Dharma

The earliest transmission of the Dharma in Tibet can be associated with the rule of three great Dharma kings, who ensured that the teachings of the Buddha could be accurately and completely established in their kingdom.

The first of the Dharma kings was Srong-btsan-sgam-po, who ruled in the first half of the seventh century. Determined to create the foundation for a full transmission of the Dharma, Srong-btsan-sgam-po created a constitution that accorded with the principles of the Dharma; sent his minister, Thon-mi Sambhoṭa, to India to develop a written language suitable for translating Buddhist texts; and joined with Thon-mi in translating several key works. He secured for Tibet several revered statues that carried with them the power of the enlightened lineage, and with his two Buddhist wives from China and Nepal, worked to build temples that would gentle and subdue forceful and hostile energies.

Five generations later, the Dharma king Khri-srong-lde-btsan saw that the time was right for establishing the Dharma. To found the Vinaya and Bodhisattva lineages and the transmission lineages of the śāstra tradition, Khri-srong-lde-btsan invited the great scholar Śāntarakṣita, abbot of Vikrama-śīla, to Tibet. To found the Vajrayāna tantric lineage, he issued an invitation to Guru Rinpoche, Padmasambhava, the renowned master from Oḍḍiyana.

Together, these masters worked to create the conditions that would make transmission possible. Overcoming great obstacles, they built bSam-yas, modeled after the famous monastery at Odantapurī in India. When it was finished, twelve monks were invited from Kashmir to establish the Vinaya lineage. At the same time, Tibetans undertook the intensive spiritual training necessary to become translators, in order to join with Indian paṇḍitas in rendering the sacred texts of the Dharma into Tibetan.

The main temple at bSam-yas monastery.

At this critical juncture, a great debate was held at bSam-yas in order to decide whether the Indian or Chinese form of Buddhism should be followed in Tibet. When the proponents of the Indian view, led by Śāntarakṣita's disciple Kamalaśīla, prevailed, a course of practice and understanding was established that would continue for the next 1200 years, down to the present day.

Early in the ninth century, the third of the great Dharma kings, Ral-pa-can, made certain that the great advances of earlier generations would not be lost. Under his direction, translations were completed and catalogued and a standardized terminology established, so that a firm body of knowledge could be passed on to future generations. At the same time, the king showed his subjects the proper way to respect the Dharma.

Following the time of Ral-pa-can, a period of suppression threatened the preservation of the Dharma lineage. However, thanks to the efforts of the great masters and rulers of these times, it proved possible to continue the teachings in an unbroken lineage. Even today, when the Dharma in Tibet itself is gravely threatened, the continuity of the Dharma lineages is being passed on from one generation to the next by masters who devote their full efforts to this all-important goal.

The Vinaya Lineage

The Buddha taught that the Dharma could survive only as long as there was a living

22

Ruins of Nālandā University, the famous center of learning in India.

tradition of Vinaya: the teachings that give guidance to the Sangha in how to live in accord with the Dharma. In Tibet, a single Vinaya tradition, that of the Mūlasarvāsti-vādins, has been followed since the time of Śāntarakṣita. This is due to the decision of King Khri-srong-lde-btsan, who issued a decree proclaiming that only this lineage should be followed in the Land of Snows. The wisdom of this policy was recognized by the great eleventh-century master Atīśa, who refused to introduce his own Vinaya lineage into Tibet, choosing instead to honor the insight of the great Dharma king.

Within the Mūlasarvāstivādin Vinaya transmission, which traces back to Rāhula, the son of the Buddha, three distinct lineages were successfully established in Tibet. The first of these is the sMad Vinaya,

which came to Tibet through Śāntarakṣita. The Ācārya Jinamitra, the Tibetan Cog-ro Klu'i-rgyal-mtshan, and many others translated various sections of the Vinaya Piṭaka in the eighth century, and Śāntarakṣita himself, together with twelve monks from Kashmir, ordained the first seven Tibetan monks.

During the reign of Glang Dar-ma, in the ninth century, when the Vinaya lineage was threatened, three monks from dPal Chu-bo-ri monastery, known as sMar, Rab, and gYo, succeeded in preserving its continuity. Aware that the work of the early masters would be lost if the Vinaya lineage did not survive, they loaded the necessary Vinaya texts onto a mule and fled to the west. Eventually they settled in southern A-mdo. There they ordained the great

23

master Bla-chen dGongs-pa-rab-gsal. In turn, the lineage passed through him to Klu-mes and the monks known as the 'Ten Men of dBus and gTsang'. When the time was right, these monks succeeded in restoring the lineage in central Tibet and in every other part of the land.

The sMad Vinaya lineage continued to flourish in eastern Tibet and elsewhere. The eminent seventeenth-century rNying-ma master Lo-chen Dharmaśrī practiced and spread the sMad teachings, which were also followed in the rNying-ma monastic college of sMin-grol-gling, founded by Lo-chen Dharmaśrī's brother, the noted scholar and contemplative O-rgyan gTer-bdag-gling-pa.

Late in the tenth century, as a new cycle of Dharma transmission began in Tibet, a second Vinaya lineage was introduced in western Tibet through the efforts of Lama Ye-shes-'od, the former king of Gu-ge who renounced the throne and became a monk out of his intense concern for preserving the Dharma. At his invitation the master Dharmapāla journeyed from India to Tibet, where he introduced the sTod lineage, also known in later times as the Pāla rnam-gsum. Thanks in part to these efforts, western Tibet during this period became a vital center for Dharma activity. Later holders of this lineage included rNgog Lo-tsā-ba Blo-ldan-shes-rab, 'Bre Shes-rab-'bar, Phag-mo-gru-pa, and bCom-ldan-rig-ral, as well as the master sGam-po-pa, (recognized as an emanation of Padmasambhava), and 'Bri-gung-skyob-pa Rin-chen-dpal, considered an emanation of Nāgārjuna.

The third and final Vinaya lineage to be established was the Kha-che lineage. Already introduced on four separate occasions into central Tibet, this lineage prospered after it was brought to Tibet early in the thirteenth century by Śākyaśrībhadra (Kha-che Pan-chen, 1127–1225).

This lineage was spread by three disciples of Kha-che Pan-chen: dPal Lo-tsā-ba Chos-kyi-bzang-po, Chag dGra-bcom, and Khro-phu Lo-tsā-ba Byams-pa-dpal. Sa-skya Pandita Kun-dga'-rgyal-mtshan (1182–1252) received this lineage, as did the great scholar Bu-ston, several masters of the Karmapa line and the revered master Tsong-kha-pa.

The Śāstra Lineages

The śāstras are the philosophical commentaries on the teachings of the Buddha. As with other transmission lineages, the śāstras are handed down from teacher to students. At the same time, the texts themselves play an especially important role, since their nature is such that they can be profitably studied by anyone able to follow their logic and reasoning.

Major elements of the śāstra tradition include the Abhidharma, Prajñāpāramitā, and Mādhyamika. Each of these traditions was first introduced at the time of Khri-srong-lde-btsan, when the first great panditas worked together closely with Tibetan lo-tsā-bas to translate these texts. Among the great lo-tsā-bas of this era were Lo-chen Vairotsana, Cog-ro Klu'i-rgyal-mtshan, sKa-ba dPal-brtsegs, and Ye-shes-sde.

As indicated by the early lDan-kar-ma catalog, the vast majority of important śāstra works (as well as almost all the Sūtras, the Vinaya, and many major Tantras) were translated either at this time or during the reign of Ral-pa-can, when teams

24

of almost a thousand translators contributed their efforts. Additional lineages were brought to Tibet in succeeding centuries, interweaving with the already existing lineages to form a rich source of knowledge and insight.

Abhidharma Among the earliest Abhidharma treatises to be translated were Asaṅga's Abhidharma-samuccaya, known in Tibet as the 'Higher Exposition', and Vasubandhu's Abhidharma-kośa, known as the 'Lower Exposition', together with its commentary. Jinamitra and the lo-tsā-bas sKa-ba dPal-brtsegs and Cog-ro Klu'i-rgyal-mtshan translated and taught each of these works. The Abhidharma lineage in Tibet branched out through three disciples of the early Abhidharma lineage holders: sNa-nam Zla-ba'i-rdo-rje, lHa-lung dPal-gyi-rdo-rje, and dBas Ye-shes-rgyal. Down through the centuries, numerous Tibetan commentaries were composed on both the Kośa and the Sammucaya.

At the time of Ye-shes-'od, early in the eleventh century, the paṇḍita Smṛtijñāna, a disciple of Nāropa, was invited to Tibet. Although he encountered great hardships, he eventually established a school for the study of the Abhidharma in Khams. His numerous disciples were instrumental in propagating the teachings of Abhidharma throughout all parts of Tibet.

Prajñāpāramitā The teachings of Prajñā-pāramitā were formally introduced into Tibet by Śāntarakṣita and Kamalaśīla in the eighth century, at a time when these texts were being widely studied in India. The spread of the Prajñāpāramitā lineage in Tibet occurred during two distinctive periods. The earlier period began with Rlangs Khams-pa, who went to India and re-turned with the One Hundred Thousand Line Prajñāpāramitā-sūtra, which he then translated and presented to Khri-srong-lde-btsan.

The scholars dBas Mañjuśrī and Nyang Indravaro also journeyed to India at this time, returning with additional manuscripts vital to the Prajñāpāramitā. Completed and edited by Vairotsana, these texts were later catalogued and placed in mChims-phu monastery. In all, some sixteen different Prajñāpāramitā Sūtras were translated at this time.

During the later spread of the Dharma, initiated by Rin-chen-bzang-po (958–1055) toward the close of the tenth century, a new transmission of the Prajñāpāramitā blossomed. Rin-chen-bzang-po had himself studied the Abhisamayālaṁkāra in India, together with its many commentaries. The great master Atīśa, who visited Tibet in the middle of the eleventh century, worked on new translations of the Prajñā-pāramitā Sūtras with several of his Tibetan students, including Khu-chen lHa-ldings-pa and 'Brom-ston rGyal-ba. The lineage of explanation that he handed down to his Tibetan disciples later became known as the Khams method.

rNgog Lo-tsā-ba Blo-ldan-shes-rab (1008–1064) studied the Prajñāpāramitā in Nepal and revised several translations. The Oral Transmission lineage then continued with the teacher 'Bre Shes-rab-'bar, who assembled the lineage of the four elder disciples of rNgog Lo-tsā-ba, as well as the lineages of Atīśa, Rin-chen-bzang-po, and those of rNgog himself.

The traditional interpretation of the Prajñāpāramitā Sūtras has been said to be based mainly on the exegeses of 'Bre and of Byang-chub-ye-shes of Ar. However, there were at least ten different schools of Prajñāpāramitā, each with its own manuals (yig-cha) for study.

The Mādhyamika Although the Mādhyamika in Tibet has chiefly followed in the lineage of the Prāsaṅgika Mādhyamika, the Yogācāra-Mādhyamika-Svātantrika line has also had a decisive influence. The basic text for this latter tradition is the Madhyamaka-alaṁkāra (dBu-ma-rgyan) of Śāntarakṣita, while the profound works of Candrakīrti and Śāntideva are among those most important for the Prāsaṅgikas. Each of the four major schools in Tibet explicates their tenets from its own particular standpoint.

In the period of the early transmission, when Śāntarakṣita himself taught in Tibet, the division between the Svātantrika and the Prāsaṅgika was not specifically introduced. The great eleventh-century rNying-ma master Rong-zom Chos-kyi-bzang-po was one of the few to make this distinction.

During the eleventh century, rNgog Lo-tsā-ba studied with the Kashmiri teacher Sajjana, who taught him the Mahāyāna-sūtrālaṁkāra, as well as several works of Maitreya. Through rNgog, who also studied the Prajñāpradīpa of Bhāvaviveka, the Svātantrika Mādhyamika became widespread, with the lineage having its center at gSang-phu monastery south of lHa-sa.

Among those who drew on these teachings were Klong-chen-pa, Jo-nang Dol-po Shes-rab-rgyal-mtshan (1292–1361), and Lo-chen Dharmaśrī and his brother, the great master O-rgyan gTer-bdag-gling-pa (1646–1714). As for the Prāsaṅgika lineage, it developed chiefly through Pa-tshab Lo-tsā-ba

and his chief disciples, who were known as the 'Four Sons of Pa-tshab'.

The Canonical Tradition

From the very outset of the Dharma transmission in Tibet, the importance of the textual tradition has been emphasized. Texts were admitted into the Canon only if their authenticity could be thoroughly verified, and every effort was made to assure that the translations into Tibetan were accurate both on the literal level and in terms of meaning. For this reason, the title of lo-tsā-ba, or translator, has always been one of the highest accolades that could be bestowed on a Tibetan master, for it was understood that in order for an accurate translation to be made, the one carrying it out had to have knowledge of the spiritual realization being transmitted.

In the early centuries of Dharma transmission, manuscripts were carefully copied by hand. During the time that the Dharma was suppressed in central Tibet in the ninth century, far-sighted masters carefully assured that the rare and precious translations made up until that time would not be lost. Thanks to their efforts, most of the early works were maintained intact. In fact, when the great master Atīśa came to Tibet in the eleventh century, he was surprised to find many authentic texts that were no longer available elsewhere in the Buddhist world.

Because the texts of the Dharma were preserved in various places throughout Tibet, it became vitally important to collect them and verify their accuracy. A number of masters contributed to this effort during the thirteenth and fourteenth centuries. At sNar-thang monastery, texts and manu-

Castle at sDe-dge monastery in eastern Tibet.

scripts were collected into the earliest full compilation of the Tibetan Canon. This collection was catalogued by Rig-pa'i Ral-gri. Later Tshal-pa Situ dGe-ba'i-blo-gros edited the old sNar-thang bKa'-'gyur. In 1320 the great scholar Bu-ston worked with the sNar-thang edition. He authenticated each text, adding more than one thousand works to the original collection. Bu-ston was the first to classify the works into the bKa'-'gyur (the teachings of the Buddha) and bsTan-'gyur (commentaries and related texts by masters of the lineage).

The first printed edition of the bKa'-'gyur was completed under the patronage of Yung-lo, a Ming dynasty emperor of China, in 1410. At least two other editions were prepared in the following two centuries. In 1692, the Ch'ing emperor K'ang-hsi sponsored another edition (the 'Peking edition'), which was supplemented in 1724 by the first printed edition of the bsTan-'gyur, for which the Fifth Dalai Lama is said to have prepared the dkar-chag. A printed sNar-thang edition of both bKa'-'gyur and bsTan-'gyur was completed in 1742, and another edition, famed for its beauty and accuracy, was completed at sDe-dge in eastern Tibet in 1744. Finally, the Co-ne edition was completed in 1773. Since that time, there have been several other editions of the bKa'-'gyur, as well as a complete Mongolian translation of both the bKa'-'gyur and bsTan-'gyur published in the middle of the eighteenth century.

The Tantra Lineages

Alone among the Buddhist cultures of Asia, Tibet succeeded in preserving intact the great tantric lineages of the Mantrayāna, known also as the Vajrayāna. Starting with the famed Vidyādharas Padmasambhava, Vimalamitra, and Vairotsana in the eighth

27

century, the early transmission of the Tantra passed through a succession of masters who would later be known as the founding fathers of the rNying-ma school. Starting in the eleventh century, a second transmission, sometimes known as the new Tantras, began, forming the basis for the gSar-ma or 'New' schools.

In the eighth century, King Khri-srong-lde-btsan established twelve meditation centers—the three most noted being mChims-phu, Yer-pa, and dPal Chu-bo-ri—for the transmission of the teachings of the Mantrayāna. Here the twenty-five disciples of Padmasambhava played an especially important role in receiving and practicing the many interweaving lineages of the Mantrayāna. In addition, Lo-chen Vairotsana actively spread the lineages of the Tantra in eastern Tibet.

During the reign of King Ral-pa-can, a clear distinction was made between two types of Sangha—the Red Sangha and the White Sangha. The Red Sangha were fully ordained monks who wore red robes in formal assemblies; the White Sangha were generally yogis or householders who wore white robes in formal assembly and often had long hair. Most of the disciples of Padmasambhava were members of the family-clan lineage of the White Sangha, which emphasized those aspects of the Vajrayāna that can be practiced under the conditions of daily life.

During the persecution of the Dharma initiated by Glang Dar-ma in the ninth century, it was relatively easy for the White Sangha to continue with its practice, which did not require formal institutions. It is said that Glang Dar-ma once received reports of a large and active group of tantric practitioners under the direction of gNubs-chen Sangs-rgyas-ye-shes, and went to investigate himself. When he arrived, gNubs at once displayed numerous feats of powerful magic, including the manifestation of a scorpion the size of a yak. This display completely intimidated the king, and thereafter he left the Sangha of tantric practitioners alone. As a result, gNubs and his followers were able to preserve numerous early translations of Dharma texts, including esoteric Tantras that would otherwise have been lost.

Toward the close of the tenth century, as temples and monasteries were once more being reestablished in central Tibet, the kings of Gu-ge in the west initiated a new series of contacts with Indian masters. The impetus for the renewed contact came from lHa Bla-ma Ye-shes 'od, a ruler of Gu-ge who resigned his throne in order to become a monk.

As Tibetans traveled to India and Indian masters journeyed north to Tibet, new Tantras became available and new transmission lineages were founded. Thus, this period is known as the time of the new transmission. Based on these new transmissions, schools of practice and study formed that soon differentiated themselves from the followers of the earlier transmission and from one another. Thus, it is at this time that it becomes appropriate to speak of the rNying-ma-pa (the 'Ancient Ones') and the gSar-ma-pa (the followers of the new traditions).

In general, both rNying-ma and gSar-ma schools shared the practice of the Kriyā, Caryā, and Yoga tantras, whose lineages of transmission are said to originate with Vajrapāṇi, Mañjuśrī, and Avalokiteśvara.

During the early spread of the Dharma, the Kriyā and Caryā Tantras were propagated by the Ācārya Buddhaguhya. During the later spread (phyi-dar) a vast number of translations of the Kriyā, Caryā, and Yoga Tantras were carried out by Rin-chen-bzang-po and his successors.

The approach of these three Tantras may be summarized as follows: The Kriyātantra emphasizes external conduct that leads toward purification through the observance of ritual actions of body and speech, guided by devotional practice directed toward the deity of the tantric mandala. The Caryātantra places equal emphasis on external ritual purity and internal meditative development. The basis for realization is viewing oneself as equal in status with the divine power, like a friend or brother. In the Yogatantra, ritual purity and similar observances are secondary; the chief focus is on meditation directed at perceiving the functioning of the mind. The individual unites with the divine, and it is the realization of this non-duality that leads to awakening. In all three forms of practice, there is an emphasis on mantra, mandala, and especially the practice of visualization, which proceeds through the two stages known as the Developing Stage and the Fulfillment Stage.

In addition to these Tantras, a more esoteric kind of tantric practice is acknowledged as well. For the gSar-ma schools, this is linked to an inner aspect of the Yogatantra, known as the Anuttarayoga-tantra. This in turn has three aspects: The Father Tantras, the Mother Tantras, and the Non-Dual Tantras. One of the principal Anuttara texts, the Guhyasamāja, was formally introduced to Tibet around the elev-enth century, when Smṛtijñāna extensively taught a major explanation lineage for this text in Khams and elsewhere in eastern Tibet. Other major Anuttara Tantras include the Cakrasaṁvara, the Hevajra, and the Kālacakra.

In the rNying-ma school, in contrast, three inner Tantras are recognized: the Mahāyoga, Anuyoga, and Atiyoga. Each of these Tantras has special texts and transmission lineages preserved only in the rNying-ma school, though the rNying-ma-pa also practice Anuttarayoga Tantras.

Within these different divisions of the Mantrayāna are found hundreds and even thousands of texts, each with its own practices, rituals, and explanations, so that the entire structure becomes extremely rich and elaborate. However, in each case the aim of such tantric practice remains wholly identical to the aim put forward in the Bodhisattvayāna: to lead all beings to enlightenment and the end of sorrow.

The Principal Schools

The rNying-ma-pa

Historically, the rNying-ma school differs from all other schools of Tibetan Buddhism in tracing its origins directly to Guru Padmasambhava and his twenty-five principal disciples, as well as the other great masters of the first transmission. In addition, the rNying-ma-pa differ from the other schools in the texts they accept as canonical. Together with the Tantras of the bKa'-'gyur, the rNyingma tradition accepts the authority of a vast body of works known simply as the rNying-ma rGyud-'bum, or Hundred Thousand rNying-ma Tantras. Finally, the rNying-ma school places special emphasis on the role of a direct transmission lineage of hidden teachings, known as gTer-ma.

Regarding its historical development, the rNying-ma school is distinguished by the tendency to emphasize the life of the layman as a valid path toward realization, as well as its acceptance of an equal role for women in transmitting the Dharma. Other Nyingma characteristics include its non-involvement in political affairs and a tendency to avoid large-scale organizations.

The rNying-ma tradition is unique in organizing the teachings of the Buddhas into nine Yānas. The first three are those known as the Śrāvakayāna, Pratyekabuddhayāna, and Bodhisattvayāna, said to originate with the historical Nirmāṇakāya Buddha. The next three are the Outer Tantras (Kriyā, Caryā, and Yoga), said to originate with the Sambhogakāya. Finally, there are the Inner Tantras (Mahā, Anu, and Ati)—said to originate with the Dharmakāya—whose human transmission lineage is held uniquely within the rNying-ma school. The Inner Tantras culminate in the three divisions of the Atiyoga, or rDzogs-chen, said to be the highest of all Dharma teachings.

The transmission of the Inner Tantras takes place through both the bKa'-ma and the gTer-ma. bKa'-ma represents the continuous transmission of the teachings of the Buddha unbounded by time or space. The gTer-ma represents the ongoing transmission of particular texts, practices, and realizations which are rediscovered after having been concealed for a period of time.

Among the early masters who played a decisive role in preserving the bKa'-ma transmission were 'the Three Zur': Zur-po-che the Elder (Zur-chen-pa Śākya-'byung-

gnas, known by the name of 'Ug-pa-lung-pa), Zur-chung-pa and sGro-sbug-pa. The former was born in 954, while Zur-chung-pa passed away in 1074, the same year that sGro-sbug-pa was born. gYung-ston-pa (1284–1365), a student of the gTer-ston Rang-'byung-rdo-rje (1284–1339) and the learned scholar Bu-ston Rin-po-che (1290–1364), was another holder of this lineage. The great scholar Rog Shes-rab-'od, another prominent bKa'-ma lineage holder, also held important lineages in the gCod and Zhi-byed systems.

Preeminent in the bKa'-ma transmission is Rong-zom Chos-kyi-bzang-po (1012–1088), who received teachings in the direct lineage of Padmasambhava, Vimalamitra, and Vairotsana. Accepted as the incarnation of a great master or Bodhisattva, Rong-zom is said to have held all the rNying-ma lineages as transmitted in the Khams tradition.

Kun-mkhyen (all knowing) Klong-chen-rab-'byams-pa (1308–1364) unified and systematized many of the bKa'-ma lineages, receiving the lineages of Rog and Rong-zom. In later times, the lineages were once more united in the accomplished gTer-ston O-rgyan gTer-bdag-gling-pa (1646–1714), both a teacher and disciple of the Fifth Dalai Lama, who held the entire body of bKa'-ma teachings and practices.

'Jigs-med-gling-pa, the direct spiritual son of Klong-chen-pa through visionary experiences, was another great master of the bKa'-ma, who gathered the texts of the rNying-ma rGyud-'bum and also systematized the work of Klong-chen-pa.

gTer-ma originate with Padmasambhava, who concealed many of the Mantrayāna teachings to be discovered and put into practice at a later time. The purpose was to create a lineage of direct realization that could counteract the tendency of the human mind to turn the Dharma into a possession of the ego. Chief among them are texts relating to the special rNying-ma teachings on the Eight Heruka Sādhanas. Guru Padmasambhava formulated eighteen classes of gTer-ma, which can include natural objects and mind transmissions as well as texts.

The first major masters of the gTer-ma tradition to appear were Nyang-ral Nyi-ma-'od-zer (1124–1192) and Guru Chos-kyi-dbang-phyug (1212–1270), who were both active in lHo-brag in the south. These two are known as the Sun and Moon, and the works they recovered are known as the Upper and Lower Treasures. Among the great gTer-stons of succeeding centuries are Rig-'dzin-rgod-ldem, whose compiled gTer-ma are known as the Northern Treasures (byang-gter). The five gTer-stons known as the Five Kings are Nyang-ral Nyi-ma-'od-zer, Guru Chos-dbang, rDo-rje Gling-pa (1346–1405), Padma-gling-pa (1450–1521), and 'Jam-dbyangs-mkhyen-brtse (1820–1892).

In the nineteenth century, the major discoveries of many of these great gTer-stons were collected by 'Jam-mgon dKong-sprul Blo-gros-mtha'-yas (1813–1899) in the sixty-two volume Rin-chen-gter-mdzod. Innumerable other teachings not contained in this collection also exist.

The first major rNying-ma monastery to be founded after bSam-yas was Kaḥ-thog, established in Khams in 1159 by Kaḥ-dam-pa bDe-gshegs, who was a holder of the Zur transmission lineage. It fell into disre-

pair beginning in the fifteenth century, but was rebuilt in the seventeenth century, a time when the active interest of the Fifth Dalai Lama in rNying-ma teachings encouraged the growth of the school. The monastery was expanded in 1656 and became well-known for its scholastic and meditative achievements. It housed eight hundred monks.

rDo-rje-brag was founded in 1610 by Rig-'dzin Ngag-gi-dbang-po in the central region of Tibet. The monastery was badly damaged in 1717, along with its neighbor sMin-grol-gling, but was rebuilt in the years that followed. It held a population of two hundred monks as well as three incarnate lamas.

dPal-yul was founded by Rig-'dzin-kun-bzang-shes-rab in 1665. Located in Khams, it housed six hundred lamas. Among its major branch monasteries was Dar-thang (Tarthang) monastery, where Tarthang Tulku received his early training.

rDzogs-chen, founded in 1685 by Padma-rig-'dzin, housed over eight hundred and fifty monks, making it the largest rNying-ma monastery in Tibet. Under the patronage of the sDe-dge royal family, it had thirteen different retreat centers and was well-known for its vast range of philosophical studies.

sMin-grol-gling was founded in 1676 by O-rgyan gTer-bdag-gling-pa. It housed over four hundred monks, and was noted for its poetic and literary achievements.

Zhe-chen was founded in 1735 by the Second Zhe-chen Rab-'byams, 'Gyur-med-kun-bzang-rnam-rgyal. It held two hundred monks and was well known for its strict monastic discipline.

Although these major monasteries and others played an important role in the rNying-ma tradition, and especially in preserving particular branches of the bKa'-ma and gTer-ma traditions, the rNying-ma continued to place a strong emphasis on practice by individuals and small groups. Because they did not separate themselves in the manner of the large monastic institutions, their presence was strongly felt within the community.

Whereas in some of the later schools spiritual power tended to become linked to specific institutions and lineages, for the rNying-ma it was more closely related to the accomplishments of a particular individual, whose own special qualities or psychic attainments made him stand out and drew students to him. In consequence, there was no occasion for centralization of authority. Often this meant that individual teachers, even those who held renowned lineages or had achieved remarkable attainments, had to exert great effort to obtain support for their studies or their religious undertakings.

The bKa'-gdams-pa

Late in the tenth century, new contacts were initiated between Tibet and India. Lama Ye-shes-'od, who ruled the kingdom of Gu-ge until his decision to follow the monastic life, sponsored the visits of several Indian paṇḍitas, and also sent young Tibetans to India to study the Dharma.

A truly decisive event for the new era in the spread of the Dharma occurred with the arrival of the revered master Atīśa in western Tibet in 1042. Renowned as the greatest teacher and scholar of his day, Atīśa, the abbot of Vikramaśīla monastery,

had previously refused requests to travel to the Land of Snow, but now he acceded to the entreaties of Byang-chub-'od, the nephew of Ye-shes-'od. Until his death in 1054, he taught widely in the west and also in central Tibet, where he resided at sNye-thang, near lHa-sa.

Atīśa had been deeply impressed by the wealth of texts and the depth of knowledge that he found among the scholars and practitioners of Tibet, but he also saw a need to return to certain fundamentals of the path. He worked on translations with Rin-chen-bzang-po, composed original works for the sake of the Tibetan people, and gave instruction to several close disciples.

Atīśa's chief disciple was 'Brom-ston rGyal-ba'i-'byung-gnas, a native of dBus and former student of Smṛtijñānakīrti. After the passing of his master, 'Brom-ston made the teachings of Atīśa into the basis of a new school, which came to be known as the bKa'-gdams-pa. In 1056, 'Brom-ston founded Rwa-sgrengs monastery as a center for the new school. Other famous masters, most of whom were disciples of 'Brom-ston, included Po-to-ba Rin-chen-gsal, who founded the monastery of Po-to, gTum-ston Blo-gros-grags-pa, the founder of sNar-thang monastery (1085), gZhon-nu-rgyal-mtshan, and Khu-ston Shes-rab-rgyal-mtshan. Blo-ldan-shes-rab, known as rNgog lo-tsā-ba, is also associated with the bKa'-gdams-pa school.

Following the lead of Atīśa, the bKa'-gdams-pa placed special emphasis on direct transmission from teacher to student, in order to assure that the teachings would be accurately presented. Thus, their teachings tended to be simple and direct, and were often written in local dialects. They also made frequent use of stories and parables to communicate the meaning of the Dharma. In terms of content, they emphasized basic Bodhisattva practices grounded in wisdom and compassion, a strict monastic discipline, and the proper observance of tantric ritual. In general, they discouraged the study of Tantra for those who did not possess the proper grounding in other Dharma studies. The masters of the bKa'-gdams-pa were famed for the purity of their practice. For the most part, they did not gather in monasteries, but preferred to live as hermits, purifying their practice.

The bKa'-brgyud-pa

The lineage of the bKa'-brgyud-pa traces to the Indian Mahāsiddha Nāropa and to his teacher Tilopa. Their teachings were transmitted to Tibet by Mar-pa Lo-tsā-ba (Mar-pa Chos-kyi-blo-gros, 1012–1097), who went to India three times to obtain teachings, and also traveled to Nepal on four separate occasions, seeking further instructions.

Firmly grounded in the siddha tradition through Nāropa and through Maitri-pa, another of Mar-pa's teachers, the bKa'-brgyud-pa have always placed great emphasis on meditation and yogic practice. Just as the rNying-ma school considers rDzogs-chen as the highest teaching, so the bKa'-brgyud-pa give special importance to Mahāmudrā, which is linked in particular to Maitri-pa.

The chief lineage of the bKa'-brgyud school traces through Mar-pa's disciple Milarepa (Mi-la-ras-pa, 1040–1123). The account of Milarepa's life is well known to all Tibetans: His use of magic to destroy his family's enemies, his sufferings at the hands of his teacher, his steady faith, and

mTshur-phu, residence of the Karmapa.

his long years spent living in the high mountains of Tibet, clad only in cotton robes, singing the lyric songs of profound illumination that have made him one of the best known of all Tibetan yogis. Milarepa's life is considered inspiring proof that it is possible for anyone, no matter what his origins, to attain complete enlightenment in one lifetime.

Milarepa had two principal disciples, Ras-chung-rdo-rje-grags-pa and sGam-po-pa (known also as Dwags-po lHa-rje, for his place of birth). At Mila's request, Ras-chung-pa traveled to India to gain a deeper understanding of the teachings known as the Six Doctrines of Nāropa, which consist of six specific forms of yogic practice. Widely transmitted after his return to Tibet, these teachings enjoy fame among all schools of Dharma in Tibet.

Ras-chung-phug monastery, at the site of the meditation cave of Ras-chung-pa, disciple of Mi-la-ras-pa.

As for sGam-po-pa, who also studied in the bKa'-gdams-pa tradition, his impact was so great that the entire bKa'-brgyud school is sometimes known as the Dwags-po bKa'-brgyud. The rNying-ma-pa consider sGam-po-pa to be an emanation of Guru Padmasambhava.

After the time of sGam-po-pa, the bKa'-brgyud-pa began to divide into numerous subschools. Of these, four are considered to be major: the Kar-ma, Phag-mo-gru, Tshal-pa, and 'Ba'-rom bKa'-brgyud.

The founder of the Karma bKa'-brgyud school was 'Dus-gsum-mkhyen-pa (1110–1193), a disciple of sGam-po-pa, who became known as the first Karmapa. He built several major monasteries, including mTshur-phu and lHa-lding. His successor,

the famous Karma Pakṣi, was the first holder of an incarnation lineage to gain official recognition.

This lineage has continued to the present day; its most recent holder, the sixteenth Karmapa, passed away in 1981. The Karmapa lineage is also called the Black Hat lineage, after a hat said to have been given them by the Ḍākinīs, and worn by each Karmapa in turn.

Other great masters of this school include the eighteenth century master Si-tu Paṇ-chen, who edited the sDe-dge bKa'-'gyur and built dPal-spungs monastery, and 'Jam-dgon dKong-sprul, the nineteenth century master of both rNying-ma and bKa'-brgyud teachings, who compiled the Rin-chen-gter-mdzod.

rDo-rje-rgyal-po (better known as Phag-mo-gru, 1110–1170), another disciple of sGam-po-pa, founded the Phag-mo-gru bKa'-brgyud school, with its principal seat at gDan-sa-mthil monastery. Phag-mo-gru, who also studied extensively with the Sa-skya master Kun-dga'-snying-po, had several disciples who each formed a subschool of the bKa'-brgyud-pa (eight in all). Of these, the most significant were sTag-lung-pa, who founded sTag-lung monastery (built in 1180) and the sTag-lung school; Gling-ras-pa Padma-rdo-rje, considered to be the founder of the 'Brug-pa tradition (together with his disciple gTsang-pa-rgya-ras); and 'Brug-rgyal-skyu-ra Rinpoche, the descendant of a long line of rNying-ma siddhas, who founded the 'Bri-gung school. In later centuries several of these schools figured in the struggles for political power that gripped central Tibet.

The Tshal-pa bKa'-brgyud-pa were established by Bla-ma Zhang-g.yu-brag-pa (1123–1192), a student of one of sGam-po-pa's disciples, who founded Gung-thang monastery. Finally, the lineage of the 'Ba'-rom bKa'-brgyud-pa trace to Dar-ma-dbang-phyug of 'Ba'-rom, founder of 'Ba'-rom monastery, and also a direct student of sGam-po-pa.

The Sa-skya-pa

The Sa-skya-pa trace their lineage to the famed master 'Brog-mi Lo-tsā-ba, who also taught Mar-pa Lo-tsā-ba before the latter went to India. 'Brog-mi (d. 1074) spent thirteen years in India studying with the great masters Śāntipa and Gayādhara. While there he learned the teaching known as 'Path and Fruit' (lam-'bras), which had been put forth by the Mahāsiddha Virūpa on the

basis of the Hevajra Tantra. The Lam-'bras teachings would later become the central doctrine of the Sa-skya school.

The actual founder of the Sa-skya school was 'Brog-mi's student 'Khon dKon-mchog-rgyal-po (1034–1102), who in 1073 founded the monastery that gives the school its name, choosing a site said to have been previously consecrated by the sage Atīśa. dKon-mchog-rgyal-po traced his ancestry to 'Khon Phal-po-che, a minister of Khri-srong-lde-btsan, and to his brother 'Khon Nāgarakṣita, one of the first Tibetan monks ordained by Śāntarakṣita and a student of Padmasambhava. The generations that followed were skilled and devoted followers of the rNying-ma teachings. More so than other major schools of Buddhism in Tibet, the Sa-skya school has maintained a very close connection to the clan of its founder.

'Khon-mchog-rgyal-po's son, Kun-dga'-snying-po (1092–1158), was the first of the five great masters of the Sa-skya school. He was renowned for mastery of the Hevajra Tantra, which has always had special significance in the Sa-skya school, and was considered an incarnation of both Avalo-kiteśvara and Virūpa. In addition to studying with several great masters, he had a direct vision of Virūpa, who remained with him for one month, imparting teachings.

The next two great Sa-skya masters were both sons of Kun-dga'-snying-po. bSod-nams-rtse-mo (1142–1182) was a noted scholar who helped systematize the new Tantras. His younger brother, Grags-pa-rgyal-mtshan (1147–1216) wrote numerous commentaries and medical treatises, as well as historical works.

The next in this lineage was Kun-dga'-rgyal-mtshan (known by the title Sa-skya Paṇḍita, 1182–1251), a grandson of dKon-mchog-rgyal-mtshan, said to be an incarnation of the Mahābodhisattva Mañjuśrī. He composed renowned works of logic, and was the first Tibetan to defeat Indian paṇḍitas in debate.

The last of the five great masters was 'Gro-mgon chos-rgyal (also known as 'Phags-pa, 1235–1280), the nephew of Sa-skya Paṇḍita and great-grandson of dKon-mchog-rgyal-mtshan. A noted author in many fields, 'Phags-pa accompanied his uncle to the court of the Mongol emperor; later he returned there and established with the emperor a relationship of teacher and patron.

In addition to Sa-skya monastery itself, Zhwa-lu monastery, founded by lCe-btsun Shes-rab-'byung-gnas in 1040, also became an important early center for the Sa-skya-pa. It was here that the great fourteenth century scholar Bu-ston, who is usually linked to the Sa-skya school, organized and edited the Tibetan Buddhist Canon.

In later centuries, sDe-dge monastery in Khams, built in the fifteenth century by the renowned master Thang-stong-rgyal-po, became a center for learning. Its printing house for the publishing of texts was known throughout all Tibet.

Eventually two subschools were formed within the Sa-skya tradition. The Ngor school was founded by Ngor-chen Kun-dga'-bzang-po (1382–1456), who in 1429 founded Ngor monastery (E-wam-chos-ldan). The Tshar-pa school was established by disciples of the great master Tshar-chen Blo-gsal-rgya-mtsho (1502–1566).

The dGe-lugs-pa

The founder of the last of the major Tibetan schools was rJe Tsong-kha-pa (1357–1419). Born in the Tsong-kha province of A-mdo, Tsong-kha-pa was trained as a boy by the bKa'-gdams-pa master Chos-rje-don-grub-rin-chen, who personally sought him out on the basis of a prophecy and took the boy with him to bDe-ba-can monastery in sNye-thang. He also received precepts from the Third Karmapa, Rol-pa'i-rdo-rje.

After his early years of study, Tsong-kha-pa traveled to central Tibet, where he is said to have studied with more than fifty great masters. Well-versed in the major śāstra traditions and in the new Tantras, he gave special weight to the Guhyasamāja and to the Kālacakra Tantra, which he studied according to the tradition of the Jo-nang-pa and that of Bu-ston Rinpoche.

After many years of retreat, Tsong-kha-pa had a final visionary realization in 1398. Thereafter he dedicated himself to teaching and writing and to laying a basis for transmitting what he had understood. He is known especially for four major events: Restoring a famous statue of Maitreya, clarifying the basis for Vinaya practice to a vast assembly of thousands of monks, founding the sMon-lam, the great Festival of Prayers that was held annually in lHa-sa beginning in 1409, and founding the great monastery of dGa'-ldan, which was completed in 1410.

Tsong-kha-pa set forth a single, unified course of study in his masterwork, the Lam-rim-chen-mo, composed at a retreat site near Rwa-sgrengs monastery. This text has guided practice in the dGe-lugs tradition since that time. His two principal dis-

Bla-brang monastery, northeastern end. This monastery housed nearly 5,000 monks.

ciples were rGyal-tshab-rje and mKhas-grub-rje, who successively became the abbots at dGa'-ldan. Since that time, the abbot of dGa'-ldan has been considered the spiritual head of the dGe-lugs-pa school.

The three most important monasteries of the dGe-lugs-pa, all located near lHa-sa, are dGa'-ldan, 'Bras-spung, founded by 'Jam-dbyangs-chos-rje in 1416, and Se-ra, founded by Byams-chen-chos-rje in 1419. Each was among the largest monasteries in Tibet, functioning almost as a small city, and able to accommodate between four thousand and nine thousand monks. Other famous dGe-lugs-pa monasteries include Chab-mdo, located in Khams and founded by Byams-chen-chos-rje in 1437, bKra-shis-lhun-po, founded by dGe-'dun-grub in 1447, sKu-'bum, located in A-mdo at the site of Tsong-kha-pa's birth, and Bla-brang bKra-shis-'khyil in A-mdo. The largest of all the dGe-lugs-pa monasteries was Ri-bo dGe-rgya-gling in Mongolia, which housed 27,000 monks in eleven colleges.

The dGe-lugs-pa came to place a strong emphasis on the monastic Sangha and on the study of authoritative texts. The colleges of the major monasteries developed their own textbooks that were used as basis for study, and a carefully graduated program of study over many years was required for advanced monks. In both their studies and their monastic organization, they emphasized a hierarchical structure that made their institutions strong and well able to provide for the monks who resided within them. In their approach to the teachings, they tended to separate study of Vinaya, Sutra, and the Śāstras from study of the Tantra. Completion of the lengthy program of studies in the former area was normally a prerequisite for beginning intensive study of the Tantras. There was a strong focus on the works of Tsong-kha-pa: Just as the Lam-rim-chen-mo formed the basis for the study of the Sūtrayāna, his sNgags-rim-chen-mo formed the basis for studies in the Mantrayāna.

Other Schools

At various times after the tenth century, great teachers founded traditions that for a time existed as schools in their own right. In the course of time, these traditions were

bKra-shis-lhun-po, the seat of the Paṇ-chen Lama, the chief dGe-lugs-pa monastery in gTsang.

reabsorbed into the major schools, contributing to the vast array of teachings preserved in the Vajrayāna.

The Zhi-byed school was founded on the basis of teachings brought to Tibet by the great South Indian master Pha-dam-pa Sangs-rgyas, the founder of Ding-ri monastery, who visited Tibet on five separate occasions in the latter part of the eleventh century. Among the teachings of this school were the practices of gCod, a powerful tantric practice that was transmitted in particular through the yoginī Ma-gcig slab-sgron, who had numerous disciples throughout Tibet. The practices of gCod, aimed at cutting directly through the obscuration of the self, were eventually taken up by several schools; in particular the rNying-ma and bKa'-brgyud. Pha-dam-pa

Sangs-rgyas continues to be honored as one of the most powerful of the Indian siddhas to visit Tibet, while Ma-gcig is one of Tibet's most famous female teachers.

Also in the eleventh century, the great yogi 'Khyung-po-rnal-'byor (b. 990) studied with Naropa's sister Niguma, an accomplished siddha who passed on to him her own lineage of special practices. Later Khyung-po, who is said to have been a student of Bon before converting to Buddhism, founded Zhang-zhong monastery in gTsang, where these teachings and others were passed on.

In the fourteenth century, 'Ba'-ra-pa rGyal-mtshan-dpal-bzang built on the foundation established by 'Khyung-po-rnal-'byor to found the Shangs-pa school. The school no longer survives independently and nowadays is sometimes described as a major division of the bKa'-brgyud-pa. Shangs-pa teachings have been assimilated into other schools, particularly the rNying-ma and the dGe-lugs-pa.

The Jo-nang-pa school, named after the Jo-mo-nang monastery in gTsang, was founded by the great Dol-bu-pa (Dol-po Shes-rab-rgyal-mtshan, 1292–1361). However, its lineage goes back to Yu-mo Mi-bskyod-rdo-rje, a revered teacher of the Kālacakra Tantra. Mi-bskyod-rdo-rje's insights into the nature of śūnyatā led him to develop an interpretation of this profound doctrine that is usually called gzhan-stong (other-emptiness), in contrast to the usual view based on rang-stong (own-emptiness). His student, Kun-spang-thugs-rje-brtson-'grus, founded Jo-mo-nang monastery, which became a chief center for those doctrines. Dol-bu-pa and his disciples propagated the special teachings of the Jo-nang-pa widely throughout central and eastern Tibet.

Because their views ran counter to fundamental tenets of certain other schools, the Jo-nang-pa became the only Tibetan school ever to be suppressed due to their unorthodox views. Although the school ceased to exist in central Tibet, it remained active in east Tibet until very recent times, maintaining the important monastery of Shar-'dzam-thang in 'Gu-log. This lineage produced some of the greatest scholars of Tibet, including the unsurpassed seventeenth century historian Tāranātha.

The Mahāsiddha O-rgyan-pa (1230–1304), a master of the Karma and 'Brug-pa bKa'-brgyud schools, established a famous teaching tradition that is sometimes also considered a separate school. O-rgyan-pa was a disciple of the second Karmapa, and also a disciple of rGod-tsang-pa. From the latter he received Mahāmudra teachings that enabled him to reach a stage of deep insight. He traveled to the sacred land of Oḍḍiyana, where he attained profound realization through teachings imparted to him by Vajravārāhī. O-rgyan-pa's lineages have passed into several schools, where they continue to be practiced and transmitted by accomplished masters up to the present day.

The great medical college of lCags-po-ri, founded by the Fifth Dalai Lama and located on one of the twin hills of lHa-sa.

The Culture of Tibet

For twelve centuries the people of Tibet have followed the way of the Dharma. Guided by the teachings of the Buddha, they developed one of the great civilizations in world history. Until recent times, Tibet had maintained unbroken a way of life that supported and sustained the very highest potential in human beings.

Throughout its recorded history, Tibet has been primarily a society of farmers, nomads, and monks. Great cities, which elsewhere have served as the foundation for civilization, played a far less important role in Tibet. For example, the estimated population of Lhasa in 1959 (excluding the residents of the great monastic universities) was only 40,000.

Religion stood at the center of every aspect of Tibetan life. It was quite common for at least one son in each family to enter the spiritual path, and by some estimates, as many as twenty to twenty-five percent of the male population lived as part of a religious order. The number of nuns, although smaller, was also extensive.

It was in those monasteries that the tradition of learning and scholarship was fostered, leading to remarkable attainments in virtually every field of knowledge. Outside the monasteries, people for the most part lived simple lives. Although there was an active and respected merchant class, it has been estimated that some eighty percent of Tibet's lay population farmed the land of the river valleys. Of the rest, many lived as nomads, grazing herds of yak and sheep in the high grasslands.

Because the land of Tibet is so rugged, it is easy to imagine that life there is full of great physical hardship, making each day a struggle to survive, but this is not so. The people of the Land of Snows love their land deeply, and consider it the most beautiful place on earth.

41

Although winters in most of Tibet are long and severe, life in the sheltered river valleys offers all the basic necessities. In some areas there is an abundance of fruits such as apricots, peaches, pears, small apples, raspberries, and walnuts, and almost every area has its own regional delicacies. For instance, in 'Gu-log a special delicacy is droma, peanut-sized tubers that grow wild and can be collected in both spring and autumn. Red in color, they are very sweet, and taste something like yams.

Even though the climate of Tibet might seem harsh to many Westerners, the Tibetan people are well-adapted to their environment. It has often been noted with wonder by Western travelers that Tibetans may go barefoot for short distances in the snow, and that nomads often prefer to sleep outside their tents even in the midst of winter. Nomads from the highlands regard the relatively mild climate of lHa-sa as dangerous to the health, due to its excessive heat, and take care not to linger there when summer approaches.

Tibet is the highest inhabited land on earth. Some nomads live at elevations of 17,000 feet and more. Since most regions lie above the timberline, there are few trees, and this has naturally had an effect on all aspects of life, from how people build their houses to how they cook their food. Tibetan nomads rely on dried yak dung for fuel. Indeed, they have learned to make use of the yak as a multipurpose animal: a beast of burden and a source of food, clothing, shelter, and many other daily necessities of life.

Due to the high altitude, the Tibetan diet is limited in its variety. Barley and meat figure prominently in the diet, together with fruits grown as regional specialties and different types of milk products such as yogurt and cheese. Salted tea mixed with butter is a steady source of nourishment. A large churn for making butter is an essential item in each household, and Tibetans sometimes drink as many as forty or fifty cups of buttered tea each day.

Tibetans seemed to thrive on this diet, and until very recent times starvation was unheard of. Though the people were certainly poor by the standards of the Western world, almost everyone had enough to live a simple, healthy life.

Tibetans have always emphasized living in harmony with the environment. For example, there are areas of Tibet rich in mineral resources and precious gems that Tibetans never mined, for they considered that doing so would disturb the delicate balance between humanity and nature. Each mountain, each spring, and every other landmark in Tibet was regarded as the abode of a spirit or god, worthy of respect and veneration. Every region had its favorite stories about the beings that inhabited its mountains, canyons, and other power places. The alienation from the environment that plagues Western societies and is gradually spreading through the whole of the world would be incomprehensible in traditional Tibetan culture. For the people who lived there, Tibet was like a vast world in itself, a cosmos alive with powerful forces and rich with unexplored wonders.

The love of nature was interwoven with love of Dharma. Human beings had a specific role to play in expressing the Dharma in the world of nature. Prayer flags flew everywhere in Tibet, hung from

42

Maṇi stones, deposited by travelers, marked Tibetan highways and passes.

trees and from lofty peaks. Prayer wheels were powered by rushing streams and by the wind as well as by human hands, and stupas were sometimes carved directly out of the rock.

At each mountain pass there were countless stones placed as offerings in gratitude for a safe crossing, and throughout the land there were Maṇi Walls: stones placed along the way that were carved with mantras and prayers. In this way, the land itself became a kind of embodied prayer, manifesting the intention of the people to enact in their own lives the profound teachings of the Buddha.

Tibetans loved to travel. Some caravans could have as many as a thousand travelers, together with 10,000 yaks, mules, and horses. Since travel could be dangerous, most travelers preferred to join in such caravans, which offered mutual protection. Often merchants, pilgrims, and monks would travel together. On the other hand, there were many wandering yogis who journeyed from place to place on their own, as well as monks who traveled in smaller groups. With steep mountains a part of almost every trade route, journeys were slow and difficult to accomplish. A journey from east Tibet to lHa-sa could easily take six months, or more than a year for the round trip.

The Place of Religion

As everyone knows, Tibet has been deeply religious for more than a thousand years. The folk religion, which focused on the divine quality of the landscape, was deeply important in the lives of the people, and Bon, the religion of Tibet before the coming of Buddhism, continued as an active force, though it had come increasingly to resemble Buddhist practice. Above all else, however, there was the Dharma. Tibetans considered themselves a deeply fortunate people, for they were watched over and protected by the Bodhisattva Avalokiteśvara. The land was alive with special power and guarded by the forces of the Dharma. Indeed, there was perhaps no place better suited to practice the teachings of the Buddha than the Land of Snows. Thus, practice entered into every aspect of life, shaping each action. A symbol of this was the prayer wheel that so many Tibetans carried, as well as the mantras that many Tibetans said continuously throughout the day.

Those who lived the monastic life were considered especially fortunate, for they had the special opportunity to bring the whole of their lives into perfect harmony with the Dharma, something that was considered extremely difficult amidst the cares and concerns of daily life.

Monks lived in various ways, depending on the school to which they belonged, their own background and degree of attainment, and the tradition of their own monastery. Monks were closely associated with their monasteries, so that a Tibetan meeting a traveling monk would not ask what school he belonged to, but rather what monastery he came from.

There were thousands of monasteries throughout Tibet, most quite small, but some with thousands of students. Typically a young boy or girl would enter the religious life at the age of about seven or eight, but not take full vows until the age of eighteen or twenty. In special circum-

stances, an individual might become a monk at any time.

In the early training of a monk, there was a strong emphasis on memorization. It was not unusual for a monk to learn thousands of pages of texts by heart, starting at a very young age. Western visitors to monastic schools sometimes commented that the dominant sound was of monks, in groups and individually, reciting out loud texts that they were engaged in memorizing. Often monks studied on their own in this way for much of the day, for they knew that they would have to face examinations in which they would be asked to recite from memory a text chosen at random. Debate was used extensively as a way of training monks in logic, argumentation, and clarity of mind. At the same time, devotional practice was also strongly emphasized, and monks were encouraged in the Mahāyāna ideal of dedicating their every action to the welfare of all beings.

Young lamas were trained to preserve the Tibetan heritage of knowledge through strict discipline. Even though they did not understand the profound texts they were memorizing, their efforts stood them in good stead, for when the time came to study the meaning of the Buddha's teachings, they found that they already knew the key works by heart.

A typical monastic schedule began with morning services at 4 A.M. Classes might last through 9 P.M. Though not all monks continued with their studies, those with special aptitude and responsibilities would maintain a focus on study throughout their lives. Perhaps it is this kind of discipline that accounts for the fact that a country with a small population was able to produce one of the richest literatures of any culture that the world has ever known.

A Great Tradition of Knowledge

Devoted to the teachings of the Buddha, the monks and nuns of Tibet, together with other accomplished masters, pass from one generation to the next the accumulated knowledge of the past. The starting point for this sacred heritage is the word, both written and spoken. Tibetan script was developed for the express purpose of translating Buddhist texts, and its language (usually classified by linguists as part of the 'Tibeto-Burmese' language group), is well-suited to transmitting the Dharma. Monosyllabic, it offers both great flexibility and precision at the same time, and the study of its grammar helps shape the mind toward clarity of thought. Though the spoken language has changed gradually over time, the classical language in which the early translations are recorded has remained the written language of the Dharma, and texts composed in the ninth century can still be read today.

Classical Tibetan is considered a sacred language, and learned treatises were written on the mystical meaning of each letter of the alphabet. No scrap of paper containing script was ever discarded; instead it was burned or buried.

Each school has its own distinctive way of presenting the three general divisions of training. The first of these is study and practice of the Vinaya, guidelines for behavior that stabilize the mind and promote well-being, making it possible to enter fully into study of the meaning of the Buddha's teachings. The second is study and practice

A turn of this giant prayer wheel set in motion the entire bKa'-'gyur and bsTan-'gyur.

of the Sutrayāna, teachings that develop insight and foster the intention to benefit to all beings. The third is study and practice of the Mantrayāna, in which the focus is on the development and completion stages of visualization and the accumulation of merit and wisdom, making use of skillful methods to reveal every situation to be a teaching.

Each of these divisions contains a wide range of subjects for intensive study; for example, in the Sutrayāna there are five topics for advanced study: logic and epistemology, Vinaya, Abhidharma, Madhyamaka, and Prajñāpāramitā. It takes years of intensive study to arrive at an in-depth understanding of even one of these topics.

Such learning does not remain only theoretical, for it is integrated with the insights that come from practice. Before intensive study begins, monks complete preliminary practices that make use of meditation, concentration, mantra, and visualization to refine body, speech, and mind. In this way, the mind is purified of obstacles to understanding from the outset, and set on the path of Dharma.

The fundamental texts for study of the Dharma were compiled in the fourteenth century as the bKa'-'gyur (the teachings of the Buddha) and bsTan-'gyur (commentaries and related texts by great masters). Editions of the bKa'-'gyur were first published in the fifteenth century, and the entire Buddhist Canon was first printed in the eighteenth century.

Arts and Sciences

Tibet produced scholars of remarkable versatility and depth. Art, science, medicine, logic, astrology, divination, history: No subject accessible to human faculties went undeveloped. Westerners familiar with the range of work carried out by some of the great masters of Tibet repeatedly express amazement at their encyclopedic knowledge in fields as diverse as metaphysics, geography, metallurgy, history and astrology. In addition, Tibetan monasteries preserved historical records of many kinds, and through the centuries great historians have drawn on these materials to compose works that reveal the unfolding of Tibetan culture over time.

Side by side with these scholarly written traditions, the oral culture of the people flourished. The creations in this realm did

The Co-ne woodblocks of the bsTan-'gyur in 209 volumes filled two large rooms.

not necessarily take Buddhist themes as their subject. They include collections of proverbs, as well as the witty and often irreverent songs sung as part of contests and celebrations, or that simply circulated among the public. There were also well-known cycles of tales, as well as the epic of Ge-sar, the national saga of Tibet, which was sung by bards throughout the land. One written version of the Ge-sar epic runs to twenty-four volumes.

Other forms of artistic creation in Tibet included the famous lama dances, stately pageants in which every step was choreographed. In addition, Tibet was renowned throughout the world for its sculpture and painting. Skillfully blending the art forms of India, China, Kashmir, and Central Asia, Tibetan craftsmen gave them a unique flavor. Painters and sculptors carried out their work as a religious practice. Relying on the guidelines set forth in treatises that insisted on a careful iconometry, they formed various schools of painting and sculpture. Their works rank among the great religious creations of world history.

A field of knowledge in which Tibet gained special prominence was medicine. As early as the seventh century, doctors trained in the Greek tradition came to the court of Srong-btsan-sgam-po. Teaching lineages established at that time and later have continued to modern times.

Medical training took at least eleven years, starting with the memorizing of thousands of pages of texts and leading on to diagnosis and treatment. Tibetan physicians developed subtle methods of diagnosis unknown in the West, and their research on herbal remedies led to the discovery of thousands of natural substances whose efficacy was proved repeatedly. Great medical colleges were built in and near lHa-sa; at the Departments of Pharmacology maintained in these colleges more than 2,000 different medicines were prepared. According to some accounts, the most complex contained as many as 165 ingredients.

A Natural Way of Life

Most Tibetans lived simply, governed by the rhythms of nature. The power of the environment was always present before the people. Villages might tend to be clustered close together, but then would come vast, uninhabited vistas, stretching for twenty

miles or more. And always there was the brilliant blue of the mountain sky, the penetrating power of the sun, and the ethereal beauty of the moon and the stars.

Attuned to natural rhythms, Tibetans treated birth and death as a part of life that could be readily integrated with daily activity. At the same time, the Tibetan view of nature extended beyond the materialistic view of the West, and so it was considered quite normal to seek advice and guidance from lamas and other holy persons with regard to many practical decisions, such as when to plant crops or whether to undertake a journey. An infant usually had its name bestowed by a lama (though the child's name might change due to significant events or on entering the monastery). Spiritual teachers were also consulted in the case of illness, which was always considered to have psychological and spiritual components. For this reason, physicians trained in Dharma as well as in medical knowledge.

The ceremonies that centered around death were considered especially important, for this was a way to help guide the consciousness of the individual who had died toward greater realization. Burial was most often in the open air, for it was considered beneficial that the body of the one who had died be used to feed other beings. Cremation was usually reserved for religious teachers, while in special cases burial in the earth or in water might be considered appropriate.

Most Tibetans lived in small villages. Village houses tended to be substantial, built of brick and stone to withstand the fierce winters. The usual pattern was for houses to have an inner courtyard, and the

Monks spend many months learning the intricate steps of the lama dances, which require great physical agility.

houses of the well-to-do might have three to four stories, with animals housed on the ground level. A typical house would be built facing south, to take advantage of the sun. The kitchen was at the center. Every house would contain a small shrine, and in addition the well-to-do might have a separate chapel.

The nomad tribes lived in tents made of yak hair that had been soaked, beaten, and squeezed repeatedly to provide good insulation. The tents were usually quite large, and nomads carried their belongings in large chests, moving them from camp to camp. As in the villages, each encampment was guarded by fierce mastiffs. So well developed was this way of life that from the times of the early kings onward, certain rulers and chiefs would establish tent cities, living for a time in one part of their realm and then moving elsewhere.

Throughout Tibetan society, women enjoyed a position of autonomy. Women could own property and inherit real property, and they often managed family finances. Their equality had been guaranteed under Tibetan law since the time of the Dharma kings.

The family is a dominant institution in Tibetan culture. Families are linked to clans, and the great clans have played a dominant role in Tibetan history. Clan lineages can be passed down through the father ('bone lineage') or the mother ('blood lineage'). The ties between uncle and

48

nephew are also important, and the ties among brothers are especially strong.

The actions of each individual reflect on the clan, while the individual's role as a member of the clan helps shape his own sense of identity. In the religious sphere, too, the clans have sometimes played an important role, linked to the transmission of a specific lineage of teachings. All the members of a clan are considered to be related, and marriages are always to individuals outside the clan.

In different areas of Tibet, different forms of marriage were practiced. Monogamy, polyandry, and polygamy were all known, though the latter appears to have been the most rare. Weddings were often played out in the form of a mock kidnapping, though the wedding itself was preceded by months of courtship, in which the families of the man and woman to be married exchanged gifts, observing a careful protocol.

Family land usually passed to the eldest son, though this was not a firm rule. It was unusual for land to be divided among brothers, for this meant that the family would be split apart.

Although Westerners tend to think of Tibet as isolated from the outside world, this perception is based chiefly on political events of the last century. Tibet has always enjoyed active interchange with the countries that surround it. Tibetans are well-known as traders, and the merchant caravan was a well-established part of the rhythm of Tibetan life.

Products produced domestically and available for trade included wool and yak hides, as well as meat and salt gathered from the great salt lakes. Wool was the largest export, together with salt, borax, and pharmacological products, for Tibetan medicine was famed throughout large parts of Asia.

Tibetan crafts were also well-known and traded within Tibet and with neighboring lands. Crafts such as carpet weaving, metal work, sculpture, and painting were often handed down within a family. Different regions were well-known for their products; for instance, sDe-dge was well known for metal work, Chab-mdo for brass, rGyal-rtse for carpets, and Kong-po for painting.

Basic items for import included tea, a true staple of Tibetan diet. For the most part, items for import were luxuries such as silk brocades and delicacies to eat. Trade was often through barter, though silver and copper coins were also in use, and paper currency was introduced in 1890.

Changes under Chinese Rule

In the last three decades, the centuries-old way of life of the Tibetan people has largely come to an end. Reports by travelers who have been in Tibet during this time make it clear that the rhythms and patterns that have governed Tibetan culture have in large measure been uprooted. Following the dictates of the Communist way of thinking, the Chinese rulers of Tibet have consciously set out to put an end to the old ways. In their place, they have tried to establish a system based on the ideology that they themselves have adopted.

The most difficult aspect of this onslaught on the old ways seems to have been the systematic efforts to eradicate the influence of the Dharma. On one level this involved the wholesale destruction of temples, monasteries, statues, and other objects of religious significance.

The scope of this destruction is difficult to describe, and its effect on the people was devastating. For example, the texts of the Tibetan Canon are considered deeply sacred, but in 'Gu-log a complete set of the Canon carved in stone under the direction of mChog-sprul Rinpoche was used for paving stones. In rDza-chu-ka a famous Maṇi Wall carved by dPal-sprul Rinpoche, extending for more than a mile, was smashed and completely destroyed. At Dar-thang monastery, 500 large prayer wheels were broken apart and burned; it took several months for the flames to burn out completely.

At a deeper level, the Chinese attempted to transform the minds of the Tibetan people. They went to great lengths to convince the local population that their faith in the Dharma had been misguided, and that their teachers had betrayed them.

According to the reports of eyewitnesses, these efforts were often quite successful. Convinced that the old ways were mistaken, Tibetans themselves sometimes carried out the work of destruction and reeducation that the Chinese considered necessary. As some of the people who lived through these times have stated, these people looked like Tibetans, but inside their minds something had undergone a fundamental transformation, and they were no longer Tibetans at all.

Today these tactics are not followed so rigorously. In the past decade the campaign against the Dharma has eased considerably. Religious symbols, monastic robes, and so forth, all prohibited for more than two decades, are once more seen, and the old monasteries are being rebuilt. A few statues and religious objects successfully hidden for decades have now been brought back into the open; others are being restored or copies are being made. Still, the change is slow. One effect of the tactics used by the Chinese, well-documented in other such cases, is to destroy trust. The people learned not to be open with one another, and only in recent years have they again felt free to express themselves. Perhaps in time it will be possible to reverse at least some of the damage that has been done.

Other changes will not be easily reversed. For example, reports by travelers and reporters make clear that the Chinese army has become a major presence in Tibet. Some 500,000 troops or more are stationed in the area known as the Tibetan Autonomous Region, and the landscape has been largely transformed to accommodate their needs. Many roads have been built for military use, and new bases have been created. There are fourteen major military air fields, as well as numerous airstrips, radar installations, and (according to various published reports in India and the West) China's major nuclear base.

Another key change has been in the environment. Parts of Tibet have long been famed for the abundance of their wildlife; for example, the region of 'Gu-log in eastern Tibet was described by the noted American botanist Joseph Rock in the 1930's as 'one great zoological garden'. He described finding blue sheep, gazelles, bears, wolves, and deer. But nowadays there are few wild animals to be seen.

Western scientists who toured Tibet in 1980 reported seeing almost no large wildlife, and few birds. Many species that were once common appear to have vanished, and may be extinct.

Tibetans had evolved successful ways for living with the land; now the attempt to 'reform' those ways has had drastic and unintended consequences. For example, under the policy of collectivized agriculture, flocks of animals were herded into large enclosures, but since these enclosures were walled off with strips of sod, the result was to denude the valleys of grass, leading to massive mud slides and disrupting the natural order. In much the same way, widespread logging in the eastern regions of Tibet during the 1970's led to extensive flooding in the 1980's.

According to reports from those who live in the area, such examples could easily be multiplied. For example, in 'Gu-log men held in labor camps were sent off each morning to collect firewood; soon the supply of wood was completely exhausted. The Chinese attempted to improve agricultural yield through the widespread use of pesticides, but as these toxic chemicals made their way up the food chain, the result was to cause great damage to wildlife. In part due to such attempts, which have

now been largely abandoned, there were several years of crop failures. For the first time in memory, the Tibetan people had to cope with widespread famine.

Today food is once more available. The diet, however, has altered considerably. Potatoes, tomatoes, and cabbage are all harvested; vegetables are far more common than in the past, and the practice of eating fish has been introduced.

The Chinese have also focused on developing raw materials. Unfortunately, laws protecting scenic sites that are taken for granted in the West have never been implemented in Tibet. As a result, many of the most beautiful areas in regions such as 'Gu-log have been scarred by mining and by such projects as power plants for generating electricity, military installations, and weather stations.

The damage that has been done to the Tibetan land and to the culture of the Tibetan people is extensive. Still, the land of Tibet and its people are resilient. Many of the traditions of Tibet live on in exile, and many of the old ways of life seem to have survived this latest challenge. With the blessings of the Buddha, Dharma, and Sangha, the people of Tibet will continue to make their own unique contribution to the human community.

Tibet in Exile

When the Dalai Lama and his close supporters left lHa-sa in March of 1959 and made their way across the mountains to India, they were only the first among thousands of refugees to seek asylum from Chinese Communist rule. Today, more than thirty years later, Tibetan refugees in exile have become a part of the world scene. Through decades of hardship and adaptation, they have become a symbol of resistance and commitment, their cause known throughout the world.

The Journey Out

The earliest refugees came mainly from the central provinces of dBus and gTsang, together with resistance fighters from Khams in the east, some of whom had met and escorted the Dalai Lama on his flight. Monks from the lHa-sa area, aware of what was happening and able to organize and leave quickly, were also among the first to flee to India. Only later, as people began to understand their changed circumstances and to see what it was like to live under Chinese rule, did families begin to seek asylum in large numbers.

Often the refugees traveled in groups of several hundred or more. Whole villages or monasteries might leave at once, or it might just be a family or two that decided on the risky journey. Sometimes refugees were caught and brought back, only to try again at the first opportunity.

In some areas near the borders of Tibet, where the Chinese at first did not exercise firm control, it was a fairly easy journey, though the decision to leave was always wrenching. But more often, the way out was difficult. Frequently the escaping Tibetans had to leave in the middle of the night and continue their travels by dark. With Chinese troops patrolling the few ac-

53

cessible roads, they had to choose remote routes, often climbing through the snow over mountain passes 18,000 feet and more in height.

The Dalai Lama entered India on March 31, 1959, and was given temporary housing by the Indian government at the Birla House in the hill station of Mussoorie. In April of 1960 he shifted his operations to McLeod Ganj (Upper Dharamsala), an abandoned hill station that now became the new seat of the government in exile.

By the end of June 1959, more than 20,000 refugees had arrived in India; before the year's end, that number had tripled to 60,000. In all more than 100,000 people successfully escaped from Tibet. Many more did not survive the journey: For example, one group of 125 that made it safely to Assam said that in the beginning they had numbered 4,000; a smaller group of fifty that started for Nepal had dwindled to seven by the time they reached safety.

Most exiles came in through Assam, in eastern India, the route taken by the Dalai Lama and his party. Much of Assam is rain forest and jungle, and for the Tibetans, arriving in their thick wool chubas and high boots, fresh from the highland plateaus, the change dramatized their entry into a new world for which they had had almost no preparation.

Others came by way of Nepal (about 15,000 in the first several years), Sikkim (about 6,000), Ladakh, or Bhutan. Of the thousands who arrived in Bhutan, the government allowed about 4,000 to stay; the rest had to continue on to India, camping at night and begging for food during the day. The journey through Bhutan typically

took about a month. Although the climate and way of life in these lands resembled what the Tibetans were accustomed to, the native population was itself poor. And because the regions that bordered on Tibet were remote, it was difficult to organize relief efforts or even to track down the refugees. Thus, the physical hardships these refugees endured were as great or greater than anywhere else, and the path toward reestablishing a humane way of life often proved a steep and rocky one.

First Response

As the government of India became aware of the scope of the refugee problem, it took steps to assure that the refugees would not starve and would receive minimum shelter. Two major camps were established. One was at Missamari, ten miles from Tezpur. The other was Buxa Duar in West Bengal near the border of Bhutan, a former British prisoner-of-war camp where Mahatma Gandhi had once been imprisoned. The site at Buxa Duar consisted of 30 concrete barracks and was surrounded by a barbed wire fence: Inhospitable and ill-suited for housing refugees, it was no longer used for this purpose after the summer of 1959.

The site at Missamari, which came to be known as a transit camp, consisted of 300 bamboo barracks built as emergency shelters in the spring of 1959. Each housed at least thirty to forty refugees, and sometimes as many as a hundred people were crowded into a single barracks. The maximum population was 9,000, so it was important to process people quickly and send them to other locations. In some cases this proved disastrous; for instance, a group

54

sent from Missamari to Ladakh after just a few weeks proved too weak to make the journey, and many of the young and the aged died under the stress. Although it was never considered more than a provisional solution to the refugee situation, Missamari continued to function from 1959 to 1968; even then there were thousands who had not been relocated in permanent settlements.

The standard procedure when refugees arrived was medical inspection, disinfection, fingerprinting and questioning, and then the issuance of clothing; sometimes blue green trousers and brown bush shirts; sometimes white cotton. But this was only the beginning.

The residents of the camps faced major health problems. The water was contaminated, so that there were recurring epidemics of amoebic dysentery. The crowded quarters and unsanitary conditions, combined with the physical exhaustion and mental shock of the escapees, made them easy targets for disease. Hepatitis and tuberculosis, for which the Tibetan people had never developed antibodies, were common. There were few families in which at least one member did not fall victim to serious and often fatal illness. The old and the very young were especially vulnerable.

In addition to illness, the new refugees had to cope with injuries suffered in travel, sickness from the change in altitude, and the intense heat. An estimated eighty-five percent of the refugees were farmers or nomads, who knew only one way of life; now everything had changed. Even the diet posed a problem: The standard rations of potato curry, rice, and lentils differed radically from the Tibetan diet of barley, but-

ter, and meat, and many people found the new food difficult to digest.

Most important, the exiles had to cope with great sadness for their country and for those who did not survive the journey, and feelings of being uprooted and adrift in a strange culture. Often in the next years, individuals would seem to just give up the will to go on: Over weeks or months the life would drain out of them, and they would take to bed, never again to rise.

The refugees who left Tibet and entered Nepal could adapt more readily, for the mountain regions that bordered Tibet were strongly influenced by Tibetan culture. In a few cases, whole monasteries were able to relocate and reestablish themselves intact, but these were rare exceptions. Most escapees found themselves facing major challenges. Without land, without property, traveling through regions where everyone was struggling to survive, they could not feel at home. Some chose to enter the Kathmandu valley, braving rumors of fierce heat, but here they had to cope with a wholly alien world, and with poverty that seemed to seep through the bricks and rise up like mist from the mud streets.

In the early years in Nepal, relief efforts were left largely in the hands of a few Western agencies. More than half of the arrivals in Nepal moved on to India, where relief efforts were more organized and more could be done to help them. Eventually four refugee camps were established in Nepal; by 1985 there were twelve camps, which still held 5,000 Tibetans.

In Bhutan and Sikkim, the story was similar: Refugees did not have to cope with extreme culture shock or change in climate, but there were few resources available to help them escape a cycle of utter poverty. In Ladakh, where the refugees had more time to prepare their escape, many drove herds of animals with them. But the winter the following year was unusually harsh, and more than two-thirds of the animals, left to fend for themselves, died. In the end, the refugees who settled in Ladakh faced some of the most difficult conditions of all, living in inadequate camps for years after many other groups had been resettled.

Coping

From the beginning the refugees faced the question of how to survive. In India, basic assistance was provided by the government at a subsistence level, but it was clear that this was only a temporary measure. In Nepal, private groups took a more active role, but at first there seemed few ways to break out of wretched poverty. Many refugees had already sold off their belongings on the journey to safety, usually at far less than their true worth; now they had to depend on the efforts of others.

Plans to support and organize the refugee community were quickly developed. Already in 1959 the Dalai Lama visited the transit camp at Missamari, and in December of that year the Dalai Lama met with an audience of 2,000 Tibetans in Sarnath, where the Buddha had first taught the Dharma. He urged them to adapt to their new circumstances and to work to preserve Tibetan culture.

The initial plan developed by the Indian government in cooperation with authorities of the Tibetan government in exile was to send the refugees to the mountains of northern India to do road work. The climate was thought to be more healthy there, a major concern in light of the spread of disease in the camps. Engaged in such work, the refugees could receive a tiny daily wage of two rupees a day or less, just enough to buy the bare necessities of life.

Roadwork began within a few months, as refugees were sent off in crowded trucks to various locations. The strenuous physical labor—mainly carrying and breaking up rock—was hard work for the refugees, who were dispirited and made weak by their journeys. The work on the mountain passes was also dangerous, and there were many fatalities. Soon the Dalai Lama made special arrangements to have trained lamas removed from this work, for it was already clear that they were a precious cultural resource, and that the death of just one lama created a hole in the fabric of Tibetan culture. For others, however, the work went on, sometimes for years. This way of life had a devastating effect on family structure, for families had to be constantly on the move, and with both parents working from dawn to dusk, there was almost no supervision for small children.

Starting in 1960, the Indian authorities began looking for remote land that could be used to start more permanent settlement communities. The first major site developed for a refugee settlement was Byllakuppe, located in rolling hills 52 miles west of Mysore in Karnataka state, in south India. Although some Tibetans thought it would be better to stay in the north because of the cooler climate, it was in southern India that uninhabited land was available. The first new settlers left for Byllakuppe in December 1960. This group numbered 666; new groups of 500 at a time were sent down at six month intervals. The work started with a week-long ceremony in which monks prayed for success.

The new territory consisted of jungle so undeveloped that tigers, wild boars, and elephants were all a real danger: Constant guard had to be posted against elephants, and several fatalities were recorded. The intense heat (even in winter, temperature averaged 80 degrees) was almost too much for the Tibetans to bear, and many died. But gradually six camps were built, each intended to house 500 Tibetans. The first permanent residences were finished early in 1962, and over time twenty villages and six monasteries were established, housing 10,000 people on 5,500 acres.

The main focus at Byllakuppe, as in most other major resettlement camps, was to be on agriculture. The soil at Byllakuppe was good, but at first the Tibetans, using farming methods learned in the completely different terrain of Tibet, fared badly. Later, with technical assistance from European relief agencies, they changed their methods and crops, planting maize and ragi (a grass cereal). Gradually 77,000 fruit trees were planted, and dairy and poultry farms were established. At the same time cooperatives were formed to engage in such businesses as tractor repair and carpet weaving. By 1966 the settlement was self-supporting, and by the end of the decade it was making a substantial profit.

Later settlements took a somewhat different course, depending on where they were located. Sometimes the soil was poor; sometimes water was in short supply. Kailaspura in Kalimpong, the second colony, was established in January 1961, when

over 500 settlers arrived. Tezu in Arunachal Pradesh was established in 1962, and by 1968 about 12,000 people lived there. Other major settlements included Mundgod and Phuntsokling, in a very remote tribal area of Orissa.

According to figures of the Tibetan government in exile, by the end of the first decade, some 30,000 of the refugees had been resettled into permanent sites, including both agricultural and industrial settlements in India, Nepal, and Bhutan. Today the vast majority of Tibetans have been resettled, though there are still several thousand who work on road gangs, awaiting a more permanent solution.

Adapting

Despite the efforts made by the Tibetans in exile and on their behalf, the first few years were marked by a kind of collective numbness. In the beginning one of the hardest parts was accepting what had happened. The refugees knew that their cause was just, and they simply could not believe they would be exiled for long. In the early years, it was hard to get news of what was happening; especially in remote areas there were only rumors, and people seized on any word that suggested they might soon be able to return to their homes.

As the truth sunk in, the Tibetan people seemed to make a collective decision: They would retain their identity as Tibetans. Even today, most Tibetans in India have not sought or accepted Indian citizenship, preferring to retain their status as Tibetans in exile.

Gradually the refugees began to take stock. What did they have left; what new beginnings could be made? In the refugee settlements numerous industrial enterprises and collectives were started, aided in many cases by seed money provided through the Office of the Dalai Lama.

Side by side with such organized efforts, the refugees themselves began to find ways of generating income. In Clement Town, Dehra Dun, a 70-member drama troop was founded independently in 1960 and began touring India to raise funds to build a settlement there. These efforts proved quite successful, and a settlement was formed under the name of the Tibetan Nehru Memorial Foundation. Among the craft activities that followed were carpet weaving and wool spinning, tent-making, paper manufacture, noodle-making, and the manufacture of machinery. A shop was also established in New Delhi to market handicrafts. A monastery was started there in 1967.

One particularly successful enterprise was marketing sweaters manufactured in the Punjab. Nomadic, and good traders almost by nature, Tibetans took these and other wares to cities throughout India. It has been estimated that in the late 1960's over twenty percent of the refugee community had this as their main business.

In Nepal a different solution developed, grounded in free enterprise. With the support of several European relief agencies, the refugees started up a new industry not previously known in that country: the sale of handwoven carpets. Eventually the success of this activity was so great that most of the Tibetan community became involved in it. Today it is the second largest source of foreign currency in Nepal, and the Tibetan community, especially in the Kathmandu valley and near other tourist centers, has become relatively prosperous.

Education

From the outset, the Tibetans realized that educating their children in Tibetan culture was vital to preserving their identity as Tibetans. The first concern was for the very young children. The earliest nursery school was opened in Dharamsala in 1960, and soon formed into an important institution known as the Tibetan Children's Village. By the early 1980's the Children's Village, which also served as a kind of orphanage, had cared for a total of more than 5,000 refugee children.

For older children, there were already rudimentary attempts at education in the first transit camps. A residential school for young men was opened in Musoorie in 1960 with fifty students; other schools were opened soon in Simla and Darjeeling. In 1962 a small printing press for producing textbooks in Tibetan was founded in Lower Dharamsala. At about that time, the first printing presses for reprinting sacred texts that were in danger of being lost were also founded.

With Indian support, a total of seven residential schools as well as several other day schools were established within the first five years of exile, with about 5,000 students in all. By the early 1980's, there were some 15,000 Tibetan students in over fifty schools. For the most part, these schools have succeeded in establishing a high standard for education. Instruction in modern subjects as well as in Tibetan language, Buddhism, and Tibetan culture are all emphasized, and there is a steady effort to instill in the students a strong sense that they are heirs to a great cultural tradition.

In Nepal, twelve private schools were founded over the course of the first decade. Starting in 1971, these schools were nationalized by the government of Nepal, but in 1981 the government reversed its policy, and the Tibetan community was once more able to reopen its own schools.

Preserving Tibetan Culture

In Tibet itself, the monasteries and the community of lamas served as the unique repository of culture and learning. All formal education took place in a religious context, and normally in association with monastic institutions. Thus, founding this tradition anew was one of the highest priorities for the refugee community.

Even for the most farsighted, it was not clear that the monastic tradition could be successfully transplanted. By one estimate, Tibet had had 600,000 monks and nuns and 4,000 incarnate lamas (tulkus) before 1959; only about 7,000 monks and several hundred tulkus escaped. In a tradition where the oral lineage counted for so much, this loss seemed almost irreparable.

Yet the effort had to be made. For some who fled Tibet after the Chinese takeover, it was clear that the twelve-hundred-year-old tradition of Tibetan Buddhism itself was in danger. Like the monks who had fled the persecution of the Dharma in the ninth century, taking with them the texts of the tradition, monks and laypeople alike sought to carry out of Tibet sacred objects and statues and rare texts. The fate of the Buddhist transmission seemed to rest in their hands.

One of the earliest efforts by the government in exile to preserve the scholarly tradition was the creation in August of 1959 of a center for studies in the former refugee camp at Buxa Duar. By 1960 almost 1,500 monks (about ninety percent of them Gelugpa) were in residence and had resumed their tradition of study, debate, and religious practice.

However, this center proved to be a poor choice. Sanitary conditions were unacceptable, and there was only one medical worker. Disease took a heavy toll; by 1967 200 monks had contracted tuberculosis. Thus, plans were made for a new center, and eventually a site was selected at Sarnath, near Varanasi. Sixty lamas from all the four major schools were sent to Mussoorie for training so that they could operate the new center; of these 56 were Gelugpa, four were Sakya, two were Kagyu, and two were Nyingma. In 1968 the Central Institute of Higher Tibetan Studies was founded in Sarnath and has operated continuously since that time. Originally affiliated with Sanskrit University in Varanasi, it has operated independently since 1977.

The Tibetan Medical Center (later combined with the Center for Astrology) was founded in Dharamsala in 1961, and a school of Tibetan medicine opened in 1969. The Tibetan Music, Dance, and Drama Society (now the Tibetan Institute of Performing Arts) was founded in 1960, and a Buddhist School of Dialectics was established in 1963.

In 1971 the Tibetan Library of Works and Archives was founded in Dharmasala. Its library and museum house over 20,000 manuscripts and a permanent photograph exhibit, and among its activities are oral history projects, ongoing classes in Buddhism, an art school, and sponsorship of numerous publications, including translations into English and other languages. Similar activities are sponsored in Tibet House in New Delhi, which has a particularly fine collection of Tibetan art.

Wherever Tibetan settlements proved successful, new monasteries and temples were built. Often the local Tibetan communities have made substantial sacrifices to provide the funds for construction. The first rough temples have in many places been replaced by major structures, though of course they fall far short of what was found in Tibet.

The monasteries founded in exile have continued to follow the traditional rules of the Vinaya that guided practice in Tibet. However, there has had to be some adaptation due to the changed circumstances; for instance, monks in many communities now engage in farming or in producing handicrafts for sale, something that would never have happened in their homeland.

Early on, publishing companies and printing facilities were established to preserve and transmit the Dharma. Among these was Dharma Mudranalaya, founded by Tarthang Tulku in 1962 in Varanasi. With much effort he and his co-workers created a Tibetan typeface and learned the basics of printing. Over the course of six years Dharma Mudranalaya published some twenty major texts. Its success encouraged other lamas to establish printing facilities as well.

Today the spiritual traditions are well-established in comparison to the early

A monk reading the scriptures.

years. There are estimated to be close to 200 monasteries among the exile community, with 35 of them located in Nepal. Schools for advanced study have also been established independently in several locations. In the settlements in the south of India, monks from the major Gelugpa monasteries of Sera, Gaden, and Drepung have refounded these establishments on a small scale, and elsewhere throughout India and Nepal lamas have tried to recreate at least a modest part of the rich heritage of the Land of Snows.

Prospects for the Future

The refugee community, now in its third generation, has succeeded in maintaining its Tibetan identity. Many efforts have been made to preserve Tibetan civilization, to found monasteries, schools, and study centers, to preserve and publish texts. Great credit goes to the work of the Dalai Lama; through his blessings and abilities, much has been accomplished. He has brought Tibetan religion and culture before the eyes of the world, making people everywhere aware of Tibet's rich heritage and its existence as an independent land with a unique contribution to make to world history.

In thinking of the progress that has been made, it is important to remember the sacrifices required to bring it about. Life has been very hard for the refugees. And yet, their suffering cannot compare with that of the Tibetans who did not escape. For those who remain in Tibet, we feel great sorrow and also great admiration for their endurance and bravery. There are many heroes, true warriors fighting for the cause of the Dharma, the rights of the Tibetan people, the freedom of their country, and the preservation of the Tibetan traditions. We pray for them and remember them.

Under the circumstances that exist in Tibet at present, a generation gap is forming that will be difficult to close. Those born in Tibet in recent times have received a type of education that leaves much out of account, while creating attitudes that make spiritual values harder to understand. The knowledge of the Tibetan tradition no longer flows smoothly from family and teachers to the younger generation, for the atmosphere of practice and faith that had such a strong influence in the past is no longer available to the same degree.

The question of whether Tibetan culture can be preserved in exile likewise remains unanswered. Of all the refugees, only a relative handful were educated lamas. Many of those with the best training were already old at the time they fled, and did not survive the rigors of the first decade. Today, someone forty years old in 1959 is over seventy years of age; soon this generation will be gone.

The older generation that remains has survived the most difficult times, but they have also gone through thirty years of hardship. Although they continue with their studies and their devotion to the Dharma, it is not always possible for them to transmit to the next generation the boundless faith of the past.

In the refugee communities today, those who are now under forty-five years of age were thirteen or younger in 1959: They did not have the opportunity to learn their own culture in its original setting. Trained in the context of a secular world, many of these young people have lost contact with the Dharma. They may identify strongly with being Tibetan, but the cultural and spiritual significance of their heritage may not speak to them directly. Though they study in fine schools and monasteries, they have never had the opportunity to see their own heritage in full operation, to appreciate its value, and to live in such a culture. Most important, the younger generation has had few opportunities to see the great enlightened ones—how they live, how they study the Dharma, how they make it a reality and communicate it to others.

Without these living examples, it is hard to inspire a true depth of appreciation and faith. For this younger generation, uninformed about its own civilization, surrounded with modern culture of a very different type, there may be a real sense of uncertainty whether their heritage has value for the modern world. For them in particular, it is deeply important that they not put Tibetan culture behind them as so much baggage from the past. May they instead come to know its beauty, carrying on the knowledge traditions that sustained their parents, grandparents, and generations before them. If young people today do not know their roots—their own mother tongue, their history, the very blood and bone of their being—how can they know who they themselves are? May the young be free to discover themselves and their connections to the heartland and homeland of Tibet.

Finally, there are the people of China, who have their own great civilization to reclaim. As they search for their own identity, we hope that the Chinese people will come to understand the importance of what has actually happened in Tibet, and that the wish will form among them to belong to the international community of modern nations that respects freedom and individuality. In the long run, strength to endure and prosper derives from harmony and balance. By supporting the Tibetan people's heartfelt desire to enjoy and share their own unique way of life, China would be making a valuable contribution to world civilization and to human happiness.

Refugees of Tibet:

A Photographic Essay

Over the past thirty years Tibetan refugees have accomplished far more than seems humanly possible. The photographic images collected here present many aspects of the Tibetan people, who persevered through these challenging times, working with courage, strength, devotion, and positive energy to preserve their heritage and their unique way of life. May the enlightened lineage that has shaped Tibetan culture bring benefit to all Tibetans and to all the peoples of the world.

PART ONE

Arrival in India

"When the horse runs on wheels and the iron bird flies, the Tibetan people will be scattered like ants across the face of the earth . . ."

Padmasambhava

In the spring of 1959, Tibetan refugees began streaming over the Himalayan passes leading into Bhutan, Sikkim, Nepal, and India. They came on foot, some with horses or mules loaded with their few remaining possessions.

These people and their horses have walked for fifteen days to a month. Climbing high into the Himalayas to escape the pursuing Chinese armies, they traveled narrow trails at night or made their own paths in the darkness.

They hid from air bombardment in dark shadows in the mountain trails and in the jungles, resting by day and eating only sporadically, because no food was available. Their exhaustion shows in their faces.

Their horses too are hungry and weary after the strenuous journey.

Hundreds of people trying to escape were killed or caught and taken back; many lives were lost. Some froze in the snow-covered mountains because they could no longer walk. Elderly people collapsed and died of exhaustion or heat in the jungles. This young man is glad to have reached India safely.

These people have come to Missamari, near Tezpur, one of two major refugee camps in India established in the spring of 1959. It was built on a sandy flat near a river in the jungle.

The Indian people could scarcely believe that refugees from Tibet were streaming into their country and walking down their roads.

At Missamari, 300 bamboo barracks had been erected in two weeks as emergency shelters. Each housed at least thirty to forty refugees, and some as many as 100.

Stunned by profound culture shock, dazed by all they have been through, some people think back on the past, and wonder what the future will bring.

Many people were ill when they arrived. During the first few months, and even during the first two years, many died because of the profound changes in climate, temperature, diet, and living conditions. Old and young were especially vulnerable.

On the very first day they arrived, in the midst of the bustle and confusion, people sit still and relax. Some are exhausted and go to sleep.

The earliest refugees came mainly from Central Tibet and Kham. These people are Khampas.

Young and old protect one another.

The women had walked in heavy boots for miles without stopping during the long nights. The man at top right carries a sword.

Unloading their thick blankets and furs, some still wear the warm hats they wore in Tibet. In India, it was the beginning of the hot season.

Taking refuge in meditation, at this worst of times.

Among the refugees were monks and lamas, learned masters whose whole lives had been devoted to study and practice.

Many lay Tibetans fled carrying Dharma books, relics, and statues rather than personal belongings or family possessions. Indian soldiers stand in the background.

Monks are recognizable by their shaven heads, although many wear lay clothes.

Some people smile at adversity, while others think back on family and friends they may never see again.

Some Tibetans are picked up on the road and brought into the camp in trucks.

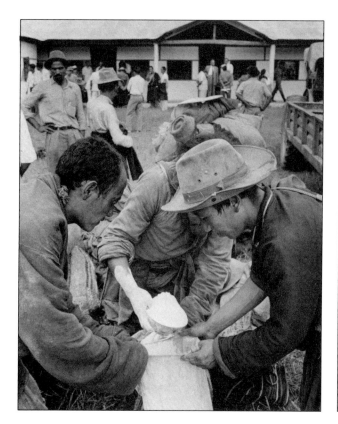

After unloading, people fortunate enough to have food pause to eat. Most have eaten little for many days.

As officials check papers, Tibetans talk among themselves and watch anxiously.

People wait their turn, wondering what will happen next. Indian soldiers stand at the back in the bottom photo.

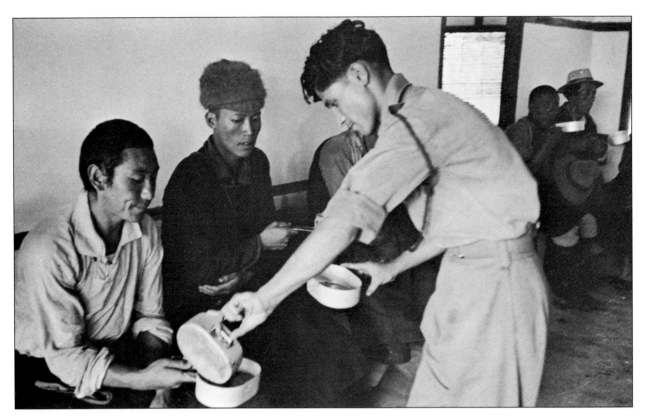

Each refugee receives an aluminum pan and something nourishing to eat. To anyone who lived through those early days, the image of those pans brings back many memories.

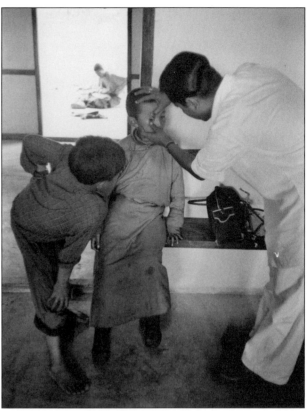

Medical inspection and disinfection was standard procedure for new arrivals.

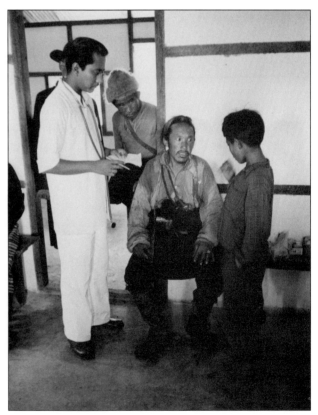

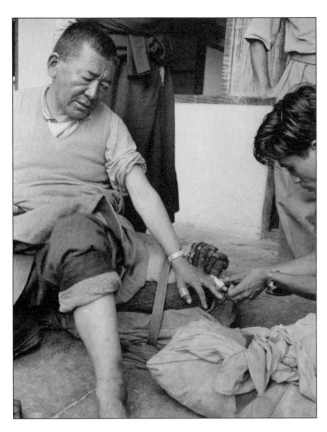
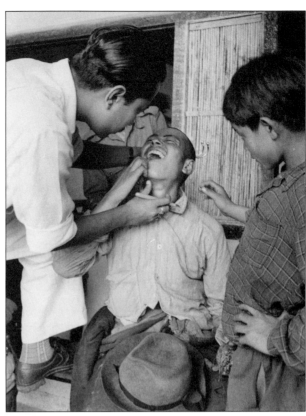

Many people were injured or suffering from hunger or exhaustion.

After the long and difficult journey out of Tibet and the shock of arriving in an alien land, it was a relief to bathe and wash clothes in the nearby river.

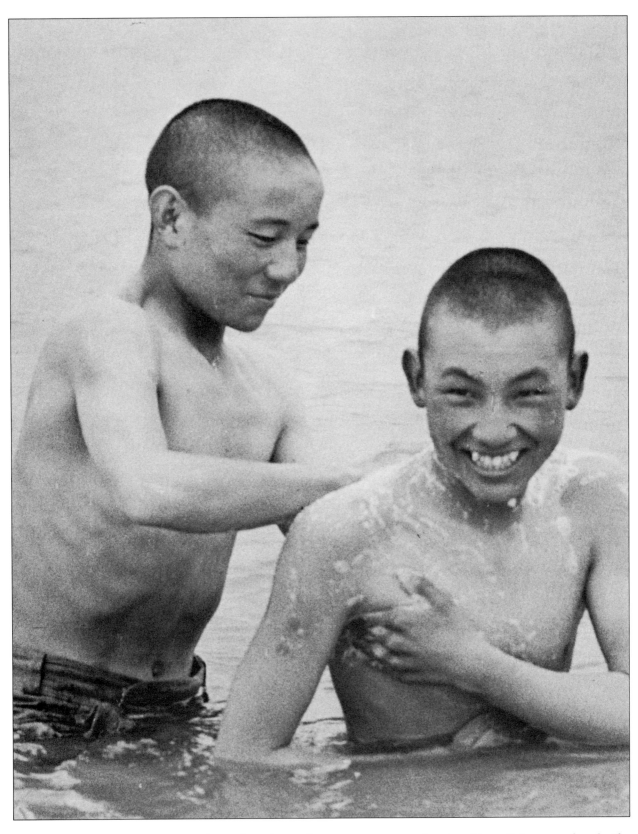

Not fully understanding what they have lost, not yet understanding this new land, the younger ones laugh and play in the water.

After bathing, the refugees wear the white cotton clothes issued by the Indian government.

Heavy blankets and clothing are laid out to dry in the hot Indian sun. Many boots and clothes could no longer be used, and had to be burned.

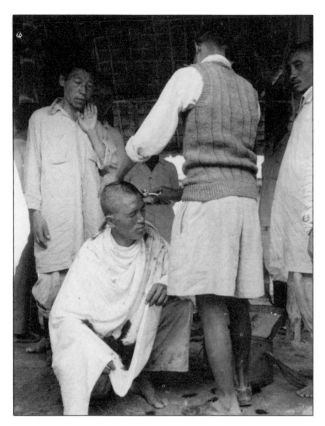
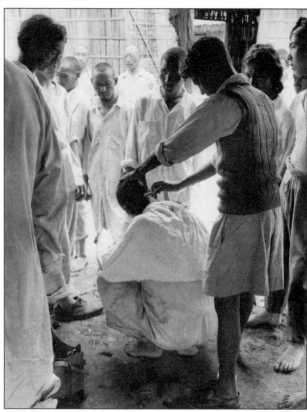

Monks and lamas have their heads shaved and prepare food inside the shacks.

In Tibet, a lama or monk would never have worn white, but in India, white was practical in the summer heat.

101

Here young monks are introduced to Western culture through an American magazine.

Even in the first days in the refugee camps, there was concern about educating the very young children. Above, children looking at Life Magazine.

Educating the children in their own culture was vital to preserving their identity as Tibetans. Here children study Tibetan (above) and English (below).

Children clap their hands to a traditional Tibetan folk song (above) and study reading and writing (below).

Not simply to survive but to contribute something of value—that was most important.

On the road crews men cut and cleared trees, women dug the roadbed, and children collected stones in baskets. Families earned about a rupee (ten cents) a day, just enough to buy rice and, once a week, a little meat and vegetables. Shopping for food, the Tibetans came in contact with the local people and were exposed to infectious diseases such as tuberculosis, against which they had no protection. Many died of disease, heartbreak, and the shock of exile.

But more separations were to come. Children could not be educated while working on road crews and some parents decided to send their children away to newly created nurseries and schools. There they and many other children who had lost their families could be cared for in this strange new land.

By the end of June, almost 20,000 Tibetans had left Tibet, and waves of refugees eventually totaling 100,000 continued to arrive in India and neighboring lands throughout the summer and fall.

The refugees waited at Missamari and the other large refugee camp at Buxa Duar, hoping that their exile in India would be short. Grieving for their homeland, for their lost children, parents, and friends, disoriented and weakened by the severe changes in culture, climate, and diet, stricken with dysentery from contaminated water and inadequate sanitation, many people died in the camps.

In an effort to stem the growing number of fatalities, and to help the refugees start a new, productive life, groups of refugees were sent to the cooler regions of northern India to do roadwork.

The strenuous physical work tested the will of many Tibetans to survive.

In the summer of 1959, the Dalai Lama visited the refugee camps. People were glad that he had left Tibetan safely and relieved that he was in their midst.

His immediate concern was to help the refugees survive and prepare them to remain in India for an extended period of time. He advised the refugees that they would have to stay in India longer than expected, and that it would be necessary to settle mentally as well as physically.

A few years earlier, the Dalai Lama had gone on pilgrimage to India to celebrate the 2,500th anniversary of the Buddha's birth, and had been welcomed with honor. Thousands of Tibetans had made the pilgrimage to India at that time, and roads and other facilities had been improved for the occasion. The Indian people associated the Dalai Lama with an uplifting of their environment and regarded him in a positive and friendly way.

The Indian government supported the Dalai Lama and the new refugees generously in whatever ways it could, while still being careful to maintain neutrality toward Communist China.

Traditional white scarves of greeting and the resounding thunder of Tibetan long horns welcome the Dalai Lama.

The banners hoisted by the crowd proclaim Tibet's autonomy and protest its takeover by the Chinese Communists.

There were uncertainties on all sides. How were the refugees to go about preserving their culture and religion in these new lands? How could they gain the skills to support themselves? How could they educate their children? Having lost their homeland, and many of their relatives and friends, could they learn to heal their suffering and pain, gather their strength, and face the enormous challenges ahead?

Even though so much had changed, the faith of the new refugee lamas remained strong and unshaken. They never forgot their daily prayers, no matter what their circumstances or conditions.

During the summer and fall of 1959, many Tibetans continued to hope that their stay in India would be short, and they would soon be able to return to Tibet. Their main focus at this point was simply trying to survive life in the refugee camps. As the months passed, and the continuing floods of refugees brought more news of what was happening in Tibet, a different truth began to settle in many people's minds: Return to Tibet was not possible at this time. In December 1959, when the Dalai Lama addressed Tibetans in exile from the Deer Park in Sarnath, his message was clear: "Do not lose heart. Take up the work of preserving our religion and our culture."

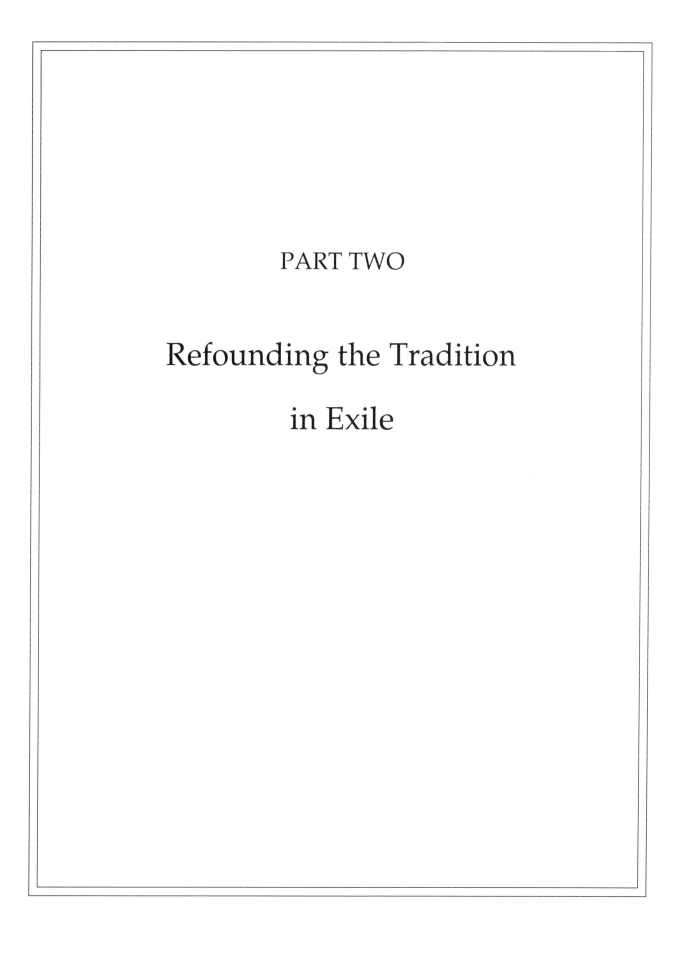

PART TWO

Refounding the Tradition

in Exile

In the 1960's and early 1970's, refugee communities gradually made progress. Settlements were established in forty or fifty places in northern and southern India, Nepal, Bhutan, Sikkim, and Ladakh. Tibetans worked industriously to grow their own food and establish self-sufficient enterprises so they did not have to rely on outside support. This determination to be self-reliant carried the refugees from the isolation of abject poverty to the creation of entire communities working together.

Sustained by devotion to the Dharma, lamas focused on preserving Tibetan culture. Schools were started and gradually monasteries were built. Printing operations were established to preserve the precious Dharma texts carried out of Tibet. Despite poverty and hardship, the refugee lamas worked diligently to maintain their unique heritage and carry on the Tibetan Buddhist tradition under most difficult circumstances.

Some refugees lived simply in huts or caves like this one.

Many Tibetans in refugee camps in border mountain regions lived in wooden shacks like these. Agriculture helped to raise their standard of living. After they became more established, some refugees were able to build more substantial homes.

Lamas join with laymen to bring in the harvest at this Gelugpa center. In the past it was not considered good for a lama to work on the land, but in India it was simply necessary to do so in order to survive, for traditional sources of support were gone, and at least some of the lamas were young and healthy. At the same time, the lamas did not give up their study and practice.

The Gelugpa lamas were often the ones who could most easily make the transition to life in India. Since their tradition was strictly monastic, they were able to leave Tibet quickly in 1959, and often did so in large groups. Thus they could transplant whole colleges from the big monasteries such as Sera and Drepung, and were able to start at once on preserving their tradition.

119

Agriculture alone could not provide an adequate livelihood for the refugees, and many settlements established crafts centers where traditional Tibetan arts were practiced. Among these was the weaving of woolen cloth and carpets.

The carpet designs, using traditional symbols in glowing colors, were uniquely Tibetan. Particularly in Nepal the Tibetan community has prospered through the successful sale of handwoven carpets.

121

The first schools for Tibetan refugee children, founded by the Dalai Lama, were opened in early 1960. Above, the Dalai Lama's mother and his two sisters, who directed the earliest nursery schools. Below, students at a small school.

The Office of the Dalai Lama placed a strong emphasis on education for the Tibetan children and with the help of the Indian government founded a number of residential and day schools. Some scholarships were also available for promising young Tibetans to attend good private schools. But it was in the monastic centers, the repositories of Tibetan culture, that Tibetan education had traditionally taken place, and gradually, as the refugee communities were more able to support themselves, small monastic schools began to grow up alongside the government-sponsored schools.

Refugee lamas began to found small monasteries and retreat centers where young monks and nuns had the opportunity to study and practice the teachings on a full-time basis.

125

126

The Dharma teachings are transmitted from one generation to the next in the close-knit environment of a small monastery. Above, young monks turn a prayer wheel.

Young monks and their teachers pose for their picture. The group at top is standing on the roof of their monastery.

128

This young monk holds a sacred text. Preserving the texts of the Tibetan Buddhist tradition was a major priority for the refugee lamas.

Here monks do traditional woodblock printing. Refugee lamas designed Tibetan typefaces and founded letterpresses in the 1960's; gradually lithograph printing facilities were developed.

Above, young lamas train in debate. The lama standing is Dzongsar Khentse; the picture was taken in 1975. Below, refugee monks making tormas (butter offerings).

In the early years at the new monastic colleges founded by the refugees, even senior students had to live in close quarters, like an army barracks. Later photos like the one below suggest how much was accomplished within the next decade.

Many monks had to work in the fields or do other physical work in order to survive, and had little leisure for study. Above, a monk cooking; below, monks beat roasted barley in sacks, part of the process of making tsampa, the national food of Tibet.

Tibetan life and culture revolves around the Dharma, and the home for the Dharma is the monastery. No Tibetan could feel settled without a strong connection to a temple or monastery. As soon as the refugees could establish themselves at all, they began to construct new temples and monasteries. In Tibet it had been common to build large monasteries, schools, and temples, but here construction strained the resources of the refugee communities. While international relief agencies aided the refugees in building houses and reclaiming land, cultural preservation was not within their scope. Often monastery or school construction had to be stopped for periods of time while the refugee communities raised additional funds.

Above, construction for a new school. Below, planning the foundation for a new monastery.

Construction in progress at the Nyingma Lama's College in Dehra Dun, India.

Plans for many of the refugee colleges included a monastery and prayer hall, living quarters for the monks, a medical clinic, and a printing press. Adjoining land was cultivated to produce food for the community.

The holy lake at Rewalsar, site of Padmasambhava's miraculous transformation. This sacred site was one of the first places where refugees built a new monastery, and later, a school.

Despite limited resources, the refugees were able to accomplish surprising things.

Starting with so little, the monks were very proud that they had been able to establish proper temples and Dharma centers.

Most of the new temples and monasteries were built in the traditional Tibetan style, and painted in beautiful, vivid colors.

All of the new monasteries and temples were built with the refugee communities' own limited funds. Construction relied heavily on personal resourcefulness.

In mountainous areas, monasteries could be built into hillsides as in Tibet, but in many areas in India, temples and monasteries were built in large open areas on relatively flat ground.

By the late 1970's, Tibetan refugees had built over 130 monasteries and temples in India and Nepal. Today the number has increased to nearly 200.

By the 1980's, some lamas were able to visit Tibet and to find the resources to help rebuild their monasteries there. Above, the rebuilt main temple of Tarthang Monastery; below, Tarthang monastery. Five hundred lamas reside there and 800 attend ceremonies.

Above left, a temple at Rahor Monastery, being rebuilt with the help of Khenpo Thupten. Right, in the background is the new shedra under construction at Tarthang Monastery. Below, Golok Tulku's monastery in Golok, Ogyen Samdrubling.

PART THREE

Tibetan Aid Project:

Penfriend Program

In Tibet the lay population had willingly and generously supported the monasteries and schools. Even in poverty and exile, the refugees continued to keep up their tradition, but their resources were far from adequate.

Refugee lamas carried a responsibility to preserve Tibetan culture, which faced the danger of extinction, and no one knew better than they did the value of the knowledge entrusted to them, and the urgency of ensuring a successful transmission to the younger generation. But most were unprepared to deal with the sudden plunge into a secular world. Ignorant of the culture in which they found themselves and lacking in worldly skills, they were often asked questions they hardly knew how to answer: "What's your job?" "Where is your family?" Lamas and monks who had devoted their entire lives to study and practice were forced to till the land or weave carpets in order to survive.

In the late 1960's, many lamas and monks still suffered from the lack of such basic necessities as food, clothing, and medical assistance, and many children needed food, clothes, and enough money to go to school. It was at this time that the Tibetan Aid Project began.

To broaden participation in the penfriend program, a flyer describing the program was written and distributed. The photo at left was used in the first TAP flyer.

TAP volunteers also provided direct aid to the refugees by gathering together food, clothing, and supplies and dispatching them to India, offering what they could in the hope that their efforts together with those made by others might amount to substantial support.

Funds were raised through all-day crafts fairs, rummage sales, auctions, concerts, film benefits, and seminars. Small dinners at the Nyingma Institute in Berkeley with slide shows presented the Tibetan culture and needs of the refugees.

In 1969, Tarthang Rinpoche suggested that each of his students at the Tibetan Nyingma Meditation Center in Berkeley, California correspond with a Tibetan penfriend, and possibly send him or her $10–15 a month.

Although this contribution was small, it could help to provide food, clothing, shelter, and medical care for senior lamas or young monks or students. Such support could also send an orphan to school, enable parents to support their children, or relieve the distress of the aged and alone.

Within a short time, Tibetan refugees seeking a penfriend began to send letters and photographs to TAP. Soon TAP had a waiting list of Tibetans of all ages and backgrounds: lamas, monks, students, orphans, aged men and women, and families.

149

Excerpts from Letters from Tibetan Refugees

"I completed my higher secondary studies and began teacher-training last year in order to serve our small brothers and sisters. But there are great difficulties. My parents can't help me as they are working on roads and depend for their livelihood on this little earning. I hope you will do your best to find a friend who can help me finish my training."

"The Doctor has said I have tuberculosis and need great treatment but for that I don't have any money to buy medicines. Thus, I have to seek your help."

"Nowadays, Manipat is very hot. A lot of people are getting sick and finding it hard to weave carpets all day long. We are most happy to have you as our friend."

"We are childless in our old age and have no one to look after us. We are facing difficulties of immense burden . . . full of prayers, I implore that this may reach the heart of a benevolent person."

"We do not have a proper house. Living in a tent is very hard during the rainy season and winter. Consequently, we have tried our best to build a house. We have erected the walls for three rooms with mud and stone, but due to lack of funds we could not do the roofing. . ."

"Our college is constructing a huge monastery of three stories of 85' by 80' by 90'. The outer walls of two stories have been completed, but due to lack of funds, our work had to be stopped. Our institution does not get aid from any country, group, or society. We solely depend on support from people like your good self. We have our litho press here, where we print religious books.

We have many poor and parentless monks here who also need financial help. The sum of $10 sent regularly each month is enough for me. In case you could help more, then kindly write to our Guru who would suggest other monks' names for sponsorship."

Tibetan Pen Friends

These people are refugees.
They need food.
They need clothes.
They need help.
Join the Pen-Friend Program.
For $15 each month,
support a Tibetan.

TIBETAN AID PROJECT
5856 Doyle Street
Emeryville, CA 94608
(415) 655-3184

[Please Take One]
We can send you the name of a lama, a child, a mother or father, a doctor or a scholar, to help save a 2000 year–old culture from dying. Donations can also be sent directly to camps and settlements and schools in Nepal, India, Bhutan and Sikkim.
☐ Please send information about the Tibetan Pen Friend Program.
☐ Please send the address of a pen friend right away.
I would like more information about other T.A.P. activities:
☐ Tax-deductible donations to the Tibetan Aid Project–Tibetan Nyingma Relief Foundation
☐ Support of a school or monastery
☐ Bringing Tibetan teachers to America.
I am enclosing a contribution of $
Name
Address
City, State, Zip

Photographs of lamas, monks, and children seeking support were combined into three large TAP posters printed at Dharma Press. These posters were distributed all over the United States, and attracted several hundred American penfriends.

151

TIBETAN PEN FRIENDS

Could you help these people? They need food and clothes.

Just $10 each month can support a Tibetan refugee.

Tibetan Pen Friends

"I am glad you all enjoyed my telling stories. You know, my dear children, even if poverty overtakes you, you can make yourself happy and that will make others happy too."

154

Children napping in an orphanage

How Can I Help a Tibetan?

Having a Tibetan pen friend is one of the best ways of helping and knowing the Tibetan people and learning their culture. The program bypasses bureaucratic middlemen and offers direct personal assistance. We have many Tibetans of all ages and backgrounds on our waiting list: lamas, monks, students, orphans, aged men and women, and families. We urge you to correspond with a Tibetan and send him or her $10–15 or whatever amount circumstances permit each month. This amount can enable an aged lama to continue his religious practice, a young monk to receive teachings before the older generation passes away, a student to go to school or enable parents to support their children.

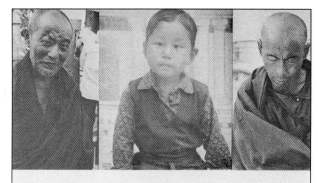

effective in promoting the Pen Friend program. TAP and Dharma Publishing co-sponsored the publication of Jataka tales for children: biograph- ical stories of the Buddha. TAP supplied half of the initial printing costs and is now receiving good dividends.

What is the Pen Friend Program?

The Pen Friend Program began with the idea that when an American and a Tibetan correspond with each other, they can help each other and mu- tually share their lives. Since Tarthang Tulku's initial suggestion that each of his students corre- spond with a Tibetan pen pal, and possibly send him $10–15 a month, more than 1000 Tibetans have found American pen friends through our Pen Friend Program.

Although posters and benefits stimulate sup- gram grows more effectively by word of mouth. Funds are equally distributed to all Tibetan ref- ugees, schools, orphanages, and camps, primarily by way of international money order. A Tibetan wrote to his American pen pal:

> I have just finished my annual examinations, and I have done perfectly well. Due to the rains and my hard efforts in studies, I am now afflicted with T.B. Should it be convenient to you, I shall be very much thankful if you could send me some

What is the Heritage of Tibet?

When Mahayana Buddhism was in danger of virtual extinction in its birthplace, India, Tibet- ans journeyed on foot across the Himalayas and managed to bring to Tibet most of the vital texts and oral transmissions from the few great Bud- dhist teachers then still living in India. Thanks to their hard work and foresight, by the time of the Muslim conquest of India in the 8th Century, Mahayana Buddhism in its most complete possible form was safely at home in Tibet.

For the next thirteen centuries (right up to 1950) Tibetans not only preserved the Mahayana Buddhist tradition but successfully made it their way of life. While other peoples began to in- creasingly busy themselves in an endless conquest of the external world, Tibetans tuned their lives to the spirit of the Dharma—to peace and compas- sion.

Have Tibetans Been Able to Adapt to New Lands?

Now uprooted from their homeland they find themselves not only in a strange world but also in a strange century. Moving from the roof of the world to the tropical plains of India, Tibetan ref- ugees have become susceptible to diseases un- heard of in their native land. Despite hardship and poverty, they have maintained their dignity as a cultured people even in exile. They have strug- gled hard and with good cheer for the past sev- enteen years to preserve their unique heritage and carry on the Tibetan Buddhist tradition under most difficult circumstances. But it is doubtful if they can carry on any further without outside help. The task of preserving their culture remains more urgent than ever before. One of mankind's greatest spiritual legacies is endan- gered and the labors of countless lamas of the past thirteen centuries will be erased if the profound and sophisticated psychological techniques in- herent in the teachings are not communicated thoroughly to the West.

What Can I Do to Help TAP?

If you're thinking about putting this away and doing something later, don't. It has been over 20 years since Tibetans left their country. They need your help now, or it will be too late to ensure that the younger generation grows strong and able to carry on their cultural tradition. Please take out a pen now and fill out the form on the next page.

Children's lives, old people's dignity and the very fabric of an entire culture are now hanging by a thread for survival. There are people to save all over the world, but there are few endangered cultures with a comparable depth of psychological and spiritual teachings. This industrious nation of people would not ask for your aid if they could prevent it. Won't you help?

Tibetan children drin

TAP volunteers also produced and distributed brochures to explain the penfriend program to Americans. Opposite: an old nun's advice to Tibetan refugee children, from a TAP brochure.

Penfriends could offer direct personal assistance to senior lamas, helping them to continue their spiritual practice.

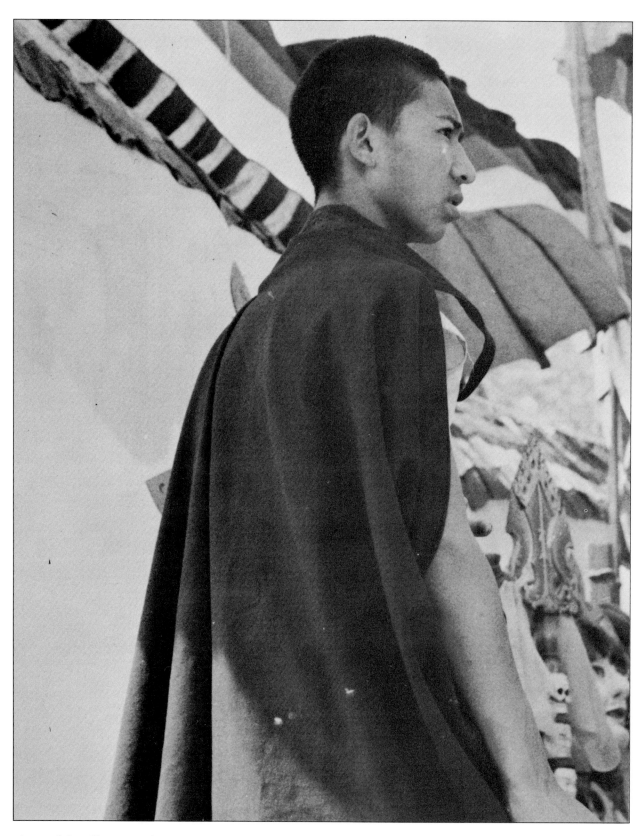

A penfriend's contribution could enable a young monk to receive teachings before the older generation passed away.

When offered aid, Tibetan monks often expressed deep appreciation for the opportunity to devote more time to study and practice.

159

For an American, having a Tibetan penfriend was one of the best ways of helping and knowing a Tibetan and learning about Tibetan culture.

It would be of great interest to know the full story of the friendships fostered by penfriends who sustained their relationship over many years.

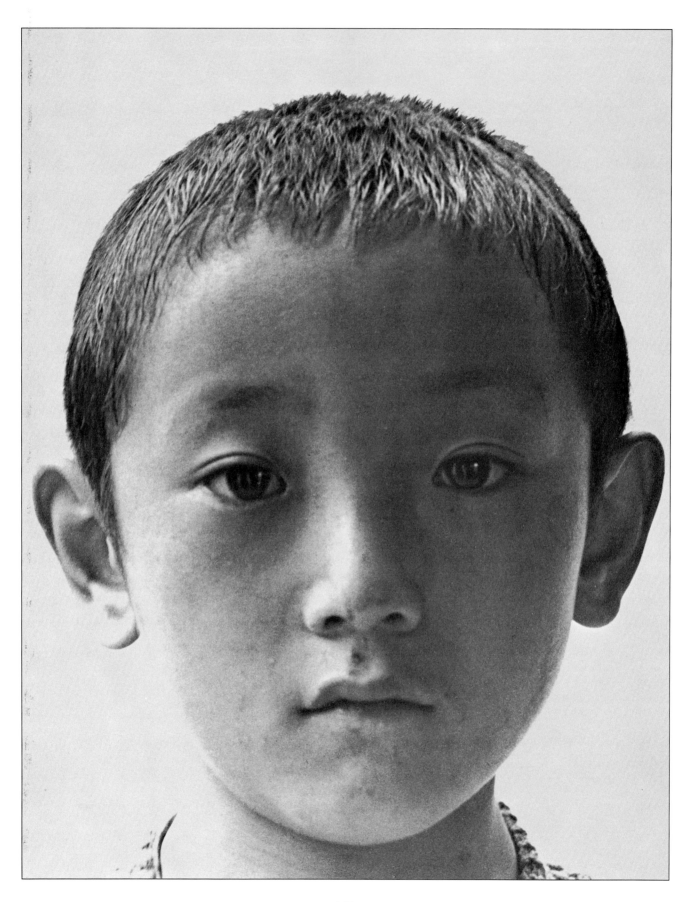

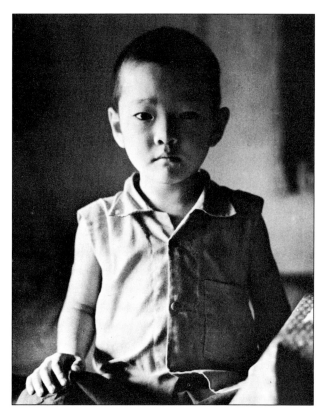

Young boys like these, who participated in the penfriend program, have grown up to become well-known teachers and heads of monasteries in India and Nepal.

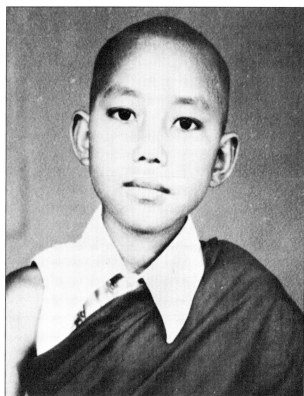

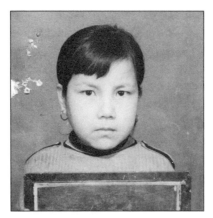

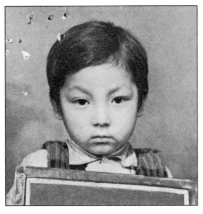

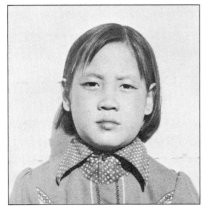

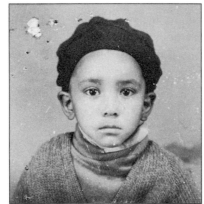

Most of these children were orphans or children from large families whose parents lacked the funds to send them to school. A contribution of $10 a month could send a child to school.

Penfriends helped these children, many of whom were born in Tibet, to build a new life in exile.

166

More than 2,400 penfriends have participated in the penfriend program to date.

In 1974, TAP set up a small clinic in Nepal, and for about six months provided direct medical support. Pencillin, skin salves, multiple vitamins, first aid kits, bandages, and dehydrated foods were distributed to the refugees, many of whom had had little care until that time.

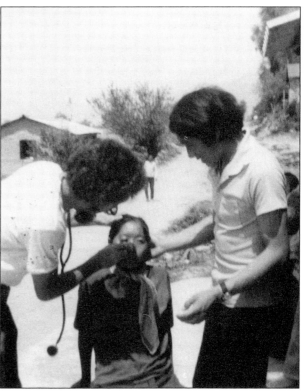

TAP doctors also provided medical assistance by visiting refugee settlements. Above, a TAP doctor examines a patient in Bir. Below, refugee monks with tuberculosis stand outside a sanatorium with their luggage.

Procession of Lama Musicians

Over the years, Tibetan penfriends sent many greeting cards to TAP to express their appreciation for the friendship and support they had received.

TIBETAN RE-SETTLEMENT PHUNTSOKLING CHANDRAGIRI
ORISSA

170

PART FOUR

Master Lamas and Monks

By the mid-1970's, with many refugees able to meet their basic needs, the task of preserving the Tibetan Buddhist tradition came to the foreground. The lamas attempting to carry on their lineages and transmit them to their students faced many obstacles. They were building schools and monasteries, but the time remaining for the few masters among the refugees to pass on their teachings was perilously short.

In 1974 the Tibetan Nyingma Relief Foundation and the Tibetan Nyingma Meditation Center began to supplement the TAP penfriend program by sending books and thanka reproductions, supporting ceremonies, and hosting visits to the United States. The photographs in this section picture some of the lamas and groups TNRF and TNMC supported. There were many lamas doing valuable work and we tried to support as many as we could. These photos, which were collected in the course of our work, are incomplete, and we have made no attempt to present the work of all the monasteries and teachers among the refugee communities. We wish we had full records and photos of all the refugee lamas, but at least these few photographs show some of the teachers and lineage holders who were working to preserve their traditions. Most of these teachers have now passed away, though the monasteries they founded carry on their traditions. TNRF and TNMC continue to support monasteries of all schools of Tibetan Buddhism in the hope that all the lineages of Tibetan Buddhism will survive and prosper.

Tarthang Rinpoche welcomes the heads of all four schools of Tibetan Buddhism: Top left, H. H. the Dalai Lama, 1979; to right, H. H. Dudjom Rinpoche, 1976; bottom left, H. H. Sakya Trizin, 1974; bottom right, H. H. Gyalwa Karmapa, 1974.

After the difficult early years, all four schools of Tibetan Buddhism established new centers in the West, and the heads of the schools began to strengthen their connection to the peoples of the West by visiting Europe and America. Continuing in the Rimey spirit of his main teacher, Jamyang Khentse Chokyi Lodoe, Tarthang Tulku, through TNMC and the Tibetan Aid Project, invited His Holiness the Dalai Lama and the spiritual leaders of the other major schools to visit the Nyingma Centers in Berkeley, California.

His Holiness Sakya Trizin, spiritual leader of the Sakya school, visited in late

August of 1974 and gave his blessing to the students.

The head of the Karma Kagyud school, His Holiness Gyalwa Karmapa, visited in October of 1974.

In 1976, two high lamas of the Nyingma lineage visited the Nyingma Centers: His Holiness Dudjom Rinpoche and His Holiness Dilgo Khentse. Both masters gave talks and blessings to the many guests.

In October 1979, His Holiness Tenzin Gyatso, the Fourteenth Dalai Lama, visited the Institute, where a public assembly was held in his honor.

His Holiness the Dalai Lama with Tarthang Tulku at the Nyingma Institute in 1979. Below, circumambulating the large prayer wheel in the Institute garden.

Following his address, the Dalai Lama visited TNMC headquarters at Padma Ling where he blessed the work on the Nyingma Edition of the Kanjur and Tanjur then in progress.

His Holiness Dudjom Rinpoche during his visit to Nyingma Centers in 1976. The pictures below show his visit to Dharma Press.

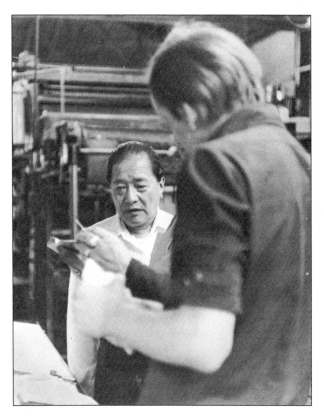

His Holiness Dudjom Rinpoche with Tarthang Rinpoche at the Nyingma Institute in Berkeley, California.

H. H. Dilgo Khentse performed the Vajrakila sadhana at Padma Ling. Below is the young seventh Zhechen Rabjam; his predecessor gave Tarthang Tulku Rinchen Terzod initiations.

178

H. H. Dilgo Khentse addresses students at the Nyingma Institute (above) and performs ceremonies with other lamas at Odiyan (below).

His Holiness the Karmapa arriving at Padma Ling in 1974, accompanied by Tarthang Tulku and monks from Sikkim.

His Holiness Sakya Trizin performing a ceremony.

181

In 1986 Tarthang Rinpoche hosted Dzongsar Khentse, the reincarnation of his teacher, Jamyang Khentse Chokyi Lodoe, at Padma Ling.

Khentse Sangyum-ma, the widow of Jamyang Khentse Chokyi Lodoe, on her third visit in 1988. This picture was taken in the Odiyan Stupa garden.

Jampal Lodoe Dzongnang Tulku (left), founder of Nyingmapa Lama's College in Dehra Dun. Formerly of Palyul monastery in Tibet, he also studied under Chogtrul Rinpoche at Tarthang monastery.

Initially Jampal Lodoe worked in Dharamsala; later, he joined with other Tibetans who had founded a drama troop able to raise funds to support the Tibetan community through its tours. Based on this source of income, he helped establish a large colony and build a monastery in Dehra Dun. He later built centers in Nepal and Taiwan; unable to continue with the center in Dehra Dun, he offered it to Mindroling Trichen. Today Khocchen Tulku carries on with the Lama's College, which continues to flourish and receives ongoing support from TAP.

LAMAS IN EXILE

Pema Norbu Rinpoche (right), a lineage holder of the Palyul monastery tradition, whose chief teacher was Tarthang Chogtrul Rinpoche.

An authoritative leader of the Nyingma school, Penor Rinpoche has worked diligently to support a large community. His monastery in Mysore, Thekchog Namdrol Shadrup Thargay Ling, is one of the largest Nyingma monasteries in India. Gulog Khenpo Tsondru and other eminent scholars were invited there to teach.

Khenpo Thupten (at front center) was originally from Mewa monastery in Kham, an important center with 1,000 students. In 1955, he and Tarthang Tulku studied together at Changma Ritro; later he came to study with Bodpa Tulku and he and Tarthang Tulku met again. In India he founded a retreat center at Pangaon Caves (above), an important site for the Nyingma tradition because of its connection to the life of Padmasambhava.

Khenpo Thupten Mewa was one of four lamas who studied together under Bodpa Tulku and were able to escape to India: Khenpo Dazer of Dzogchen monastery, Rahob Thupten, Khenpo Thupten Mewa, and Tarthang Tulku. Of these, Khenpo Dazer, a master of the Nyingma lineage, was especially instrumental in passing on major lineages in Mysore (where he had 500

students) and in Sikkim and Bhutan. In fact, he served as a teacher for these lineages for almost all the refugee lamas in India.

Bodpa Tulku (Dongag Tempey Nyima) is generally regarded as the greatest Nyingma philosopher of this century. From his teacher Kunzang Paldan, a great master who was one of Lama Mipham's three principal disciples and also a student of Patrul Rinpoche, he received the transmission of Lama Mipham's written teachings. Bodpa Tulku himself was an incarnation of Patrul. Patrul's teacher in turn studied under Jigmed Lingpa, so the lineage of transmission to this great master was very direct.

This teaching lineage has played a vital role in the transmission of Nyingma in the times since 1959.

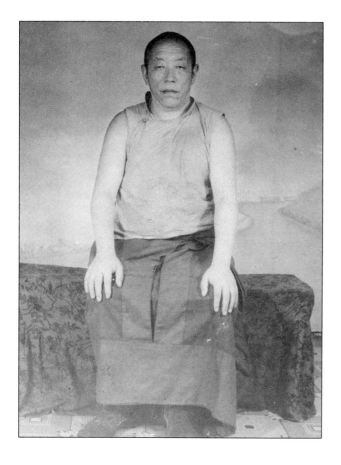

Khenpo Tsondru (left), a Nyingma lama from Gulog, a great master of the Dzogchen Nyingthig lineage. He also studied at Sera monastery, the famous Gelugpa center in Lhasa. Kongtrul Rinpoche was his meditation teacher. Unfortunately, he passed away at an early age.

Khenpo Tsondru was a great scholar and meditator and a master of the sutras and shastras, as well as of poetry, grammar, and medicine. His impact as a teacher was immense, and it can truly be said that almost all Nyingma lamas who have sought to refound their tradition since leaving Tibet are his students. Like Khenpo Dazer, he was instrumental in passing on major Nyingma lineages. Tarthang Tulku plans to publish their correspondence in the future.

Although Khenpo Tsondru was not a student of Bodpa Tulku, he was in the same lineage. Today, there are only a few left who carry this same line of teachings.

Tarthang Tulku (right) in Varanasi in 1964. A disciple of the second Jamyang Khentse Wangpo, Tarthang Tulku left Tarthang monastery while still quite young to study with great teachers from all four schools. In 1963 H. H. Dudjom Rinpoche recommended him as Nyingma representative at Sanskrit University in Varanasi. While there, he gave seminars and lectures, and founded a publishing company that reprinted twenty texts. He is shown here with Thupten Chogdrup, a learned and highly intelligent scholar of Sanskrit.

In 1968 Tarthang Tulku traveled to America, where he founded TAP, Dharma Publishing, and other operations devoted to preserving and transmitting the Dharma. His wish to memorialize the experiences of his lama friends and all Tibetan refugees is the impetus behind the present book.

Minyak Khenpo Rapgyay (far left), who held the Palyul lineage and the lineages of Chogtrul Rinpoche. He was a remarkable individual who escaped many times from the Chinese. He went first to Kalimpong, where he organized many young lamas. Then he was sent to Rewalsar, the first Nyingma monastery in India. He worked with Jampal Lodoe Rinpoche to build Ngedon Gahtsal Ling in Dehra Dun and founded Palyul Chokor Ling in Kangra, which he left in the care of Rigo Tulku.

Khenpo Rapgyay was a man of great courage, vision, integrity, and faith, and a spiritual father to his students. Through his support, he brought them great benefit.

Khorlo Lama (at right) assisted Minyag Khenpo Rapgyay, working closely with him on behalf of the Dharma and the Nyingma lineage. He resided at Rewalsar. Like too many of the leading lamas of his generation, he passed away at a young age.

186

Chusang Lama (left), from Dorje Drag monastery in Tibet, was given charge of the monastery at Rewalsar. He came originally from Minyak in Kham. He and Tarthang Tulku were close friends, but he has now passed away.

Chusang Lama was a tutor to Ngawang Zabtrang Namgyal, an important lama in the Drukpa Kagyud lineage of Bhutan.

Rigo Tulku (right), who is in charge of Palyul Chokor Ling at Kangra. This monastery was founded by Minyak Khenpo Rapgyay, who passed away in the 1970's. It has flourished under Rigo Tulku's care and leadership.

187

Lopon Sonam Zangpo (left) trained in both the Drukpa Kagyu and Nyingma traditions. His teacher was Togden Shakya Shri, a student of the great Adzom Drugpa. A highly realized master, artist, and meditator, he built several important temples and repaired the Swayambhu Stupa. He and Tarthang Tulku met at his center in Bhutan in 1958; together they visited Jamyang Khentse Chokyi Lodroe at the royal palace in Sikkim in 1959, receiving important teachings shortly before this master passed away. Afterwards, the two went on pilgrimage to India. His daughter married Tulku Thinley Norbu and their son was proclaimed the reincarnation of Jamyang Khentse.

Ngagchen Sherab Lama (right), an important Nyingma lama who has now passed away, together with his wife Pema Lhazom. Ngagchen Sherab Lama was a disciple of Dudjom Rinpoche.

*Venerable Tulku Urgyen (left), a descend-
ant of Chokyur Dechenlingpa, assisted His
Holiness the Karmapa for many years in
Nepal, working at a temple now under the
direction of the Zhwamarpa. He founded
Ka-Nying Shedrup Ling, the largest monastery in Nepal, which is now under the
direction of his son Chokyi Nyima
Rinpoche; he supervises Nagi Gompa, a
major nunnery that he also founded.*

*Sai Yung Sang De Chen (right), the wife of
Urgyen Tulku and mother of Chokyi Nyima
Rinpoche and Chokling Rinpoche, standing
in front of Asura Cave in Nepal, where
Guru Padmasambhava practiced Vajrakila
and Herukasadhana. Together with her
husband, Sai Yung Sang De Chen built a
large temple there. Recently TAP was able
to support adding a large gold spire to this
temple.*

*Sai Yung Sang De Chen played an equal
role with her husband in all of his work.
Unfortunately, this fine lady passed away
this past summer, at almost the same time
as the mother of Tarthang Tulku. When
Tarthang Tulku saw her for the last time,
shortly before her death, she said, "We will
meet another time."*

Chokyi Nyima Rinpoche (left), son of Tulku Urgyen, holds both Nyingma and Kagyu lineages, but was a student of the late Karmapa, and so is closer to Kagyu. His brother, Chokling Rinpoche, is the reincarnation of Chokyur Dechenlingpa, one of the very greatest Terma masters of the past century, whose powerful teachings are still widely practiced.

Chokyi Nyima Rinpoche is in charge of Ka-Nying Shedrup Ling in Kathmandu, Nepal, where he teaches many Western as well as Tibetan students.

Khenpo Rigdzin (right) was a student of both Khenpo Tsondru and Khenpo Dazer, and also studied at the Central Institute of Higher Tibetan Studies. In addition, he was a student of Sakya Khenpo Rinchen and Penor Rinpoche. He is now the director of the Nepal Nyingma Institute, a shedra founded by Chogtrul Rinpoche and Tarthang Rinpoche in 1989. For the past two years there have been 108 students at this shedra, all engaged in serious study of the Nyingma tradition and teachings. Khenpo Rigdzin has done very good work in making this young institution flourish.

190

Above (left), Dapsang Tulku, a Kagyu lama who founded a monastery in Kathmandu, and (right) Dzongsar Khentse Rinpoche in 1968.

Above (left), Lama Karam Singh, a student of Khenpo Thubga, who was one of the most renowned scholars in Dzachuka. On the right is Thopgay Lama, a lama of the Nyingma school.

191

Thegchok Namdrol Shadrup Thargay Ling in Mysore, Head Lama Penor Rinpoche.

Duddul Rapten Ling, a Nyingma group in Orissa, Head Lama Ripa Tulku.

Nyingmapa Buddhist Monastery, Pangaon Caves, Head Lama Khenpo Thupten Mewa.

Gyurmeling Monastery, Kangra, India, Head Lama Tulku Urgyen Topgyal.

Nyingmapa Buddhist Monastery, Rewalsar, Head Lama Lama Konchok. Khocchen Tulku is to right of center, front row. He is in the Mindroling tradition, and administers the Nyingmapa Lama's College in Dehra Dun.

Tashi Choeling, Head Lama Jedrung Rinpoche.

Chorten Gonpa, Sikkim, Head Lama Dodrup Chen Rinpoche.

Sikkim Institute of Higher Nyingma Studies, Head Lama Khenpo Dechen Dorjee.

Gyudmed Tantric University, Karnataka State, India.

This group in Mundgod, India, takes care of a Nyingma chapel within Drepung Monastery.

PART FIVE

Ceremonies and Rituals:

Preserving Tibetan Culture

As the new monasteries and schools in the refugee communities became firmly established, they could devote more time and energy to the transmission of the Dharma teachings. To support the stronger emphasis on practice and study, the Tibetan Nyingma Relief Foundation and the Tibetan Nyingma Meditation Center began to sponsor ceremonies at monasteries and schools.

Sponsoring ritual prayers and scripture readings offers blessings to all beings. At the same time, it gives substantial encouragement to the monks. It provides food and offerings for the duration of a ceremony, and supports study of scriptures and meditation practice.

The Gyalwa Kanjur Rinpoche ceremony, in which all 108 volumes of the Buddha's teachings are read aloud, is considered highly meritorious. Over the past eighteen years, TNRF and TNMC have sponsored 233 Gyalwa Kanjur Rinpoche ceremonies. Ceremonies have also included readings of the Heart Sutra, Medicine Buddha Prayers, Sitatapatra White-Umbrella Prayers, the Ye Dharma Mantra, the Manjushri Nama Sang Gyud, Sampa Lhundrup, and sadhanas to specific deities, as well as stupa painting and the printing and sewing of hundreds of prayer flags.

Ceremonies for all four schools are in some ways similar, but each school has its own distinctive approach. In an effort to help all the sects maintain their traditions, TNMC and TNRF have sponsored ceremonies in monasteries of all schools.

199

Playing traditional instruments for a religious ceremony.

Traditional offerings include butter lamps and torma. Oil is very precious and making butter lamp offerings involves considerable sacrifice on the part of the monks.

Above, Rigo Tulku presiding at a religious ceremony. Below, a ceremony at the Nyingmapa Lama's College.

Above, Penor Rinpoche stands by the altar and ceremonial seat at the beginning of a ceremony; below, during the ceremony.

Before performing the Kanjur Rinpoche ceremony, monks in procession circumambulate their monastery. Above, monks carry the woodblock prints of the sacred texts.

Kanjur readings at Pangaon Cave led by Khenpo Thupten Mewa (above) and the Tsechu Association led by Gulog Tulku (below).

Kanjur reading at the Institute of Higher Nyingma Studies in Sikkim, one of the first Nyingma shedras to be created by the refugees. It was founded by Khenpo Dazer.

Reading from the scriptures has always been a vital element in Buddhist practice.

Offerings during a ceremony at the Nepal Nyingma Shedra, founded by Tarthang Rinpoche and Chogtrul Rinpoche, and directed by Khenpo Rigdzin. Although in the first year there were only a few students, in the second and third years there were 108.

Topics of study include Abhidharma, Madhyamika, Prajnaparamita, logic, poetry, and grammar, as well as traditional rituals and skills and the intensive study of sadhanas. The results so far clearly indicate that the new shedra will be worthwhile.

Kanjur reading at Gelugpa centers: Gyuto Tantric University (above) and Gyudmed Tantric University (below).

Gyalwa Kanjur Rinpoche ceremonies at Drepung Monastery (above) and Sera Mahayana Monastic and Philosophy University (below), important Gelugpa centers.

During the Kanjur Rinpoche ceremonies at the Sakya Monastery in Mundgod (above) and the Sakya College in Dehra Dun (below).

Above, a ceremony at a Kagyu temple, led by Thrangu Tulku, a student of Zhechen Khenpo Lodro Rabsal. Below, a Kanjur Rinpoche ceremony.

Nuns and monks participate in a Kanjur Rinpoche ceremony.

214

His Holiness the late Dilgo Khentse presiding over a religious ceremony.

215

Above, a lama dance at Thegchok Namdrol Shadrup Thargay Ling in Mysore. Below, a Black Hat Dance held in Dehra Dun on the occasion of the Tibetan New Year.

Lama dances at Tashi Jong, a Drugpa Kagyu center. The dances are stately, but also require tremendous agility from the dancers, monks who spend months in training.

An outdoor ceremony.

218

At top, members of the lay community join students at the Nyingmapa Lama's College in an outdoor ceremony. Below, a religious ceremony being held for lay people, Lama Thopgyay and others presiding.

219

Preparing food for a ceremony for Golok Tulku in Darjeeling. Large numbers of people are served from the huge round pots.

PART SIX

Ceremony for World Peace

at Bodh Gaya

The Bodh Gaya Stupa, which marks the place of the Buddha's enlightenment, has been a sacred pilgrimage site for over 2,000 years. In the past, hundreds of thousands of great Enlightened Ones came to this holy place, but once Buddhism ceased to be a living tradition in its homeland, interest waned and the site was forgotten. Only in this century have Buddhists reclaimed this sacred setting and begun to build temples there.

Tarthang Rinpoche writes:
"For some years now I have felt that nothing is more important for the world today than saying prayers at the Bodh Gaya Stupa. In 1978, His Holiness Dilgo Khentse Rinpoche recited 100,000 Pranidhanaraja at Bodh Gaya at my request and with my sponsorship. In 1981, I asked His Holiness to recite 100,000 Manjushri Namasamghiti at Bodh Gaya. He was unable to participate at that particular time so Khenpo Dechen Dorje and Dodrup Chen Rinpoche led the ceremony instead. In the years since, TNMC has sponsored many offerings and ceremonies at Bodh Gaya.

"In December 1989, I visited Bodh Gaya and sponsored a twenty-five day Puja for World Peace, the Longevity of the Teachers, and the Growth of the Dharma. Head lamas, monks, nuns, and lay people from over eighteen different places attended the ceremony, some for the whole time and others for part of it. It had been twenty years since I had seen some of these people, and I appreciated very much their coming on short notice.

"Among those who attended were His Holiness Khentse Rinpoche, Penor Rinpoche and 100 monks from Mysore, Shaptrul Rinpoche and monks from Nepal, Rigo Tulku and fifty monks from Kangra, Chogtrul Rinpoche, Lahtrul Rinpoche, Khocchen Rinpoche and monks from the Nyingmapa Lama's College, Khenpo Rigdzin and eighty monks from Nepal, Khenpo Dechen Dorje and twenty-five monks from Sikkim, Tsechu Rinpoche and monks from Darjeeling, Taklung Tsetul and monks from Simla, Khenpo Thupten Mewa and monks from Manali, nuns from Beru near Dehra Dun, Zankur Rinpoche, monks from Bhutan, and others, totaling up to 600 monks on the last days of the puja.

"Many prayers were recited at the time, including 300,000 Namasamgiti and 100,000 Pranidhanaraja. In addition, TNMC sponsored 100,000 Namasamgiti recitations at five Gelugpa monasteries, including Sera and Drepung. Extensive offerings of butter lamps and candles were made each day at the Bodh Gaya Stupa and also at the Gelugpa monasteries participating in the ceremonies. Offerings of incense, fruits, flowers, tormas, and other precious items were *made daily. At the end of the ceremony, each participant received a gift of a Tibetan text.*

"In January 1991, at the second Peace Ceremony, almost 1,500 lamas and monks participated, and this year more may attend. This makes three years that TNMC has sponsored this ceremony, and we hope to continue to sponsor it in the coming years. TAP has also given funding, and Dharma Publishing has contributed thanka reproductions which were given to the participants.

"It has been hundreds of years since such beautiful ceremonies with offerings of butter lamps, candles, incense, flowers, and fruits have taken place at Bodh Gaya. The costs for sponsoring the ceremony are very high, but they are worth it. I hope that other organizations and monasteries will wish to help support this ceremony and I encourage them to do so.

"I also hope that this example will encourage others to sponsor ceremonies at Bodh Gaya throughout the year, especially in the winter when the weather is good. The different schools of Tibetan Buddhism and schools from other countries such as China, Thailand, Taiwan, Burma, and Sri Lanka could all sponsor ceremonies at Bodh Gaya and other holy sites, keeping their traditions alive and helping the Sangha to flourish as it did in ancient times. Through such offerings

at sacred places, the Buddhist teachings can prosper, generating momentum for world peace and happiness for all sentient beings.

"It is not always easy for Tibetan refugees to be able to afford to make the pilgrimage to Bodh Gaya. But if there is support from other organizations, they could be encouraged and sponsored. This seems important, for through the Tibetan refugees, the teachings of the Buddha, which were originally transmitted from India to Tibet, are returning to India, and coming to life at this great Stupa.

"In these troubled times, when people all over the world are vulnerable to confusion and despair, we cannot rely on logical approaches to bring improvement to our planet and our world. Each step of materialistic progress brings with it that much more suffering, and it seems that no day goes by without war somewhere on the planet. Compassionate prayer seems to be the only answer. There is no power greater than the power of prayer at holy places. According to ancient texts, the site of the Buddha's enlightenment can truly be considered the center of the earth. Through heartfelt prayer at the Bodh Gaya Stupa, the most holy of Buddhist places, magical changes can occur in the world."

Beyond the beliefs of any one religion,
there is the truth of the human spirit.
Beyond the power of nations, there is the power
of the human heart. Beyond the ordinary mind,
the power of wisdom, love, and healing energy
are at work in the universe. When we can find
peace within our hearts, we contact
these universal powers.
This is our only hope.

Tarthang Tulku

Remarks on the occasion of the Bodh Gaya
International Peace Ceremony, January, 1991

Bodh Gaya Stupa

During the first Bodh Gaya Peace Ceremony in December, 1989, hundreds of lamas circum-ambulated the stupa each morning before assembling for prayers.

From monasteries and retreat centers in India, Tibet, Nepal, Bhutan, and Sikkim, lamas and monks representing Nyingma and the other Tibetan schools came to Bodh Gaya.

Masters and lineage-holders, tulkus, and abbots joined with monks and nuns of all ages, chanting from morning until night, accompanied by the sounds of bells, cymbals, and horns.

Even as the gateways to freedom were opening throughout Europe, mantras resounded continuously from all sides of the Stupa, setting in motion powerful aspirations for world peace.

Offerings included beautiful butter-sculptured tormas, over 600,000 butter lamps, incense, garlands of flowers, rice, water, fruit, and fabric. Below, monks light the butter lamps.

Especially on the last day, on each side of the Stupa—north, south, east, and west—tables were laden with abundant offerings.

At sundown, the candles encircling the Stupa radiated light in all directions.

Pure light offered to the Enlightened Ones with faith and devotion.

Aware of the great value of this pilgrimage and ceremony, participants asked that it become an annual event. Above, His Holiness the late Dilgo Khentse at prayers.

Tarthang Rinpoche offering Tibetan texts to participants, including the Prajnaparamita Sutra in 8,000 lines and the Chos-dbyings-rin-po-che'i mdzod. At top left, Chogtrul Rinpoche.

At the second Ceremony for World Peace in January 1991, a time of great turmoil in the world, 1,500 lamas came together for ten days of continuous chanting and prayer.

Lamas from a hundred different monasteries and centers gathered in groups on all sides of the Stupa. Even in Tibet such a gathering of lamas would have been rare.

Hundreds of thousands of butter lamps, candles, and incandescents were lit as offerings to lighten the impending darkness and bring harmony to the hearts of all beings.

Garlands of light adorn the Stupa, carrying wishes for balance in nature and the full awakening of all human beings to peace and joy.

Exquisite tormas are offered to the Enlightened Ones. In Tibet, the major monasteries created distinctive styles of torma associated with their teaching lineages.

Concentrating on prayer at this Tara statue on the northern side fulfills many wishes. Offerings of gold leaf restored many sacred statues on the Stupa grounds.

Students from TNMC made the pilgrimage to Bodh Gaya to distribute books and thanka reproductions on Tarthang Tulku's behalf, and to help with preparations for the ceremony.

The texts offered to the sangha included the much-loved Manjushri Namasamgiti, which was chanted during the ceremony.

The compassionate ones have vowed to return again and again to aid suffering beings. Above, Sogpa Tulku (left), the reincarnation of Tarthang Tulku's father, and Pega Tulku, the brother of Tarthang Tulku. Below, Pega Tulku at the ruins of Nalanda.

Tibetan Texts Given to Bodh Gaya Ceremony Participants

December 1989
One volume, containing:
Chos-dbyings-rin-po-che'i-mdzod
gSang-ba'i-snying-po
Heart Sutra
Prajnaparamita Sutra in 8,000 Lines
sDud-pa
bZang-spyod-smon-lam

January 1991
One volume containing:
Chos-dbyings-rin-po-che'i-mdzod
Chos-spyod
Mtshan-brjod
Diamond Sutra
Thar-pa-chen-po'i-mdo
Another volume containing:
Mtshan-brjod commentaries

January 1992
Seventeen rNying-ma Tantras, 2 volumes
Seven Treasures of Klong-chen-pa, 4 volumes

Thankas Given as Gifts at the Ceremonies

January 1991
2,000 Thankas of Buddhas, Bodhisattvas, and Deities
4,000 small Guru Rinpoche cards

January 1992
25,000 Thankas of Buddhas, Bodhisattvas, and Deities

Production and shipping costs of books 1989: $20,447
Production and shipping costs of books 1991: $57,743
Production and shipping costs of books 1992: $200,000
Production costs of Thanka prints: $5,000
Total of Ceremony Texts and Thanka Gifts: $283,190

1989 Bodh Gaya Ceremony Report

Lights for World Peace
Over 600,000 butter lamps and candles: 300,000 butter lamps and 160,000 candles at the Bodh Gaya Stupa and 200,000 butter lamps and more candles at Gelugpa monasteries.

Altar Offerings
Incense, fresh fruits and flowers, butter sculpture tormas, and other offerings were made daily.

Statue Restoration
The Buddha statue in the Stupa temple was coated in gold. New brocade canopies, hangings, and yolwas were sewn and installed inside the temple and at the entrance to the Bodh Gaya Stupa Buddha room.

Transportation
Costs for 500 participants to come to Bodh Gaya. Head Lamas, monks, nuns, and lay people from over 18 different places attended the ceremony.

Tents, Housing, Land Fees, Kitchen, and Utilities
To support 500 chanters for twenty-five days.

Tea Offerings and Robes
Tea was offered to all the monks twice daily at the Stupa. New lama robes sewn and distributed to over 125 monks.

Beggars' Food and Gifts
Over 2,000 beggars were given food, money, and new cloth every other day of the ceremony.

Financial Offerings to Practitioners
To support prayers and chanting by 500-700 participants from 7 A.M. to 5 P.M. for twenty-five days.

Costs for TNMC Representatives to attend
Travel, food, and lodging for six representatives.

TOTAL COST $122,000

1991 Bodh Gaya Ceremony Report

Lights for World Peace
Hundreds of thousands of butter lamps, candles, and incandescents burning each day.

Altar Offerings
1,080 garlands of flowers, 4,000 sculptured tormas, 4,000 sticks of incense, and 100,000 cookies, fruits, and nuts.

Statue Restoration
The Buddha statue in the Stupa temple was coated in gold.

Transportation
For 1,500 monks and nuns to come to Bodh Gaya. More than 500 traveled over 1,000 miles to be present.

Tents, Housing, Land Fees, Kitchen, and Utilities
To support more than 1,500 chanters for ten days.

Food
To provide meals for 1,500 people for ten days.

Cooks' Salaries
Indian residents employed. All other organizational tasks were salary-free, including administrators, coordinators, secretaries, and purchasing agents.

Beggars' Food and Gifts
Three meals for 300 local beggars as an offering to create an atmosphere of satisfaction and appreciation and to alleviate immediate suffering.

Financial Offerings to Practitioners
To support prayers and chanting by 1,500 individuals from 7 A.M. to 5 P.M. for 10 days.

Costs for TNMC Representatives to attend
Travel, food, and lodging for six representatives at the ceremonies.

TOTAL COST $100,700

Summary of TNMC/TNRF Support for Tibetan Culture
1969 - 1991

Buddhist Canons

Seven sets of the 120 Volume Nyingma Edition of the sDe-dge bKa'-'gyur and bsTan-'gyur, together with two eight-volume catalogues, and 84 copies of the Guide to the Nyingma Edition. These Buddhist Canon editions were received by: His Holiness the Dalai Lama, Dharmasala; His Holiness Dudjom Rinpoche, France; His Holiness Penor Rinpoche, Byllakuppe, India; Tarthang Monastery, Tibet (2 sets); Khra-gling Monastery, Tibet.

Dharma Books

Over 300 volumes in Tibetan script with English translations of the Dhammapada and the Bhadrakalpika. More than 600 copies of English volumes of Crystal Mirror, Kindly Bent to Ease Us, Life and Liberation of Padmasambhava, Nyingma Annals, and Lalitavistara.

Thanka Reproductions

Thanka reproductions are printed in full color on heavy coated paper. Thanka reproductions of Buddhas, Bodhisattvas, Padmasambhava, Siddhas, Gurus, and mandalas, and protection mantras have been donated to monasteries. Over 69,597 thankas have been sent throughout the Himalayas to Head Lamas for distribution (not including 1992 gifts).

Ceremonies and Visiting Lamas

TNMC has hosted more than fifteen lamas and tulkus with entourages of one to fifteen monks or family. Visits last at least a week or more and include events such as formal meals, teachings, and excursions.

Ceremony Sponsorship

The Tibetan Nyingma Relief Foundation and the Tibetan Nyingma Meditation Center have sponsored 233 Gyalwa Kanjur Rinpoche ceremonies. Ceremonies have included prayers for the longevity of teachers, readings of the Heart Sutra, the Manjushri Namasamgiti, the Pranidhanaraja Sutra, the Ye Dharma Mantras, and sadhanas to specific deities.

Some of the Tibetan centers and individuals to whom
TNMC/TNRF/TAP has been able to offer support:

Nyingma Lamas and Monasteries

Ananda Temple
Asura Caves
Azin Rinpoche
Bodh Gaya Monastery
Byatral Rinpoche
Bumthang Tharpaling Sheda
Chatral Sangye Dorjee Rinpoche
Chusang Lama
Dalip Singh Bodh
Dapzang Monastery
Derge Khamtul
Dilgo Khentse Rinpoche
Dobzang Monastery
Dodrup Chen Rinpoche
Dojeden Gompa
Dongzong Gompa
Dorzong Rinpoche/Lama Kargyud
Duddul Gonjo
Dukpa Rinpoche
Dungsay Yonten Ghatso Rinpoche
Dzogchen Tulku
Dzongsar Jamyang Khentse
Gautama Nath
Geley Lechey
Golok Amber
Golok Tsemgon
Golok Tulku
Gonpo Tenzin
Gonpo Topgyal
Gonpo Tseten
Great Aspiration Prayers
Gyatrul Domang Rinpoche
Gyatse Tulku

H. H. Dudjom Rinpoche
H. H. Mindolling Trichen
Jedrung Rinpoche
Ka-Nying Shedrup Ling
Karwang Nyima
Khando Padma Dechhen
Khempo Rabjey
Khenpo Appey
Khenpo Dazer
Khenpo Dechen Dorjee
Khenpo Palden Sherab
Khenpo Pema Sherab
Khenpo Rigzin Dorje
Khenpo Thupten Mewa
Khenpo Thupten Rahob
Khenpo Tsewang Dongyal
Khenpo Tsondru
Khenpo Tsuden
Khentse Sangyum
Khetsun Sangpo
Khochhen Tulku
Konchok Lama
Kontrul Rinpoche
Kuna Lama
Kunga Chegpa Lama
Lama Gelong Rigzbaing
Lama Golok Jigtse
Lama Gono Topgyal
Lama Goser's Gompa
Lama Karam Singh
Lama Thembo Monastery
Lama Thimbu Monastery
Lama Tsewang

Nyingma Lamas and Monasteries

Lama Tsewang Phuntsok
Lama Yonden
Lati Tacha
Longkar Gompa
Mahabodhi Society
Maratika Retreat Center
Matikalo's Lama
Nenam Pao Rinpoche Monastery
Nepal Nyingma Institute
Ngedon Gahtsal Ling
Nyingma Mahabuddha Vihara
Nyingmapa Monastery
Nyingma Students Welfare Comm.
Nyoshul Khenpo
Payul Choktrul
Pega Tulku
Pema Jigme
Pema Lama
Pema Lhazom
Penor Rinpoche
Pema Wangyal
Pema Yangtse Monastery
Penor Rinpoche Charity Found.
Rabjam Tulku
Ralo Monastery
Rewalsar: Nyingma Buddhist Mon.
Rigo Tulku
Ripa Tulku
Dorje Namgyal
Samten Choling Monastery
Sang Ngag Tulku
Sangyay Lama
Sei Gompa
Shadar Rinpoche
Shenphen Dawa Rinpoche
Sherab Raldri
Sengedrak Tulku

Sogpo Tulku Chime Dorjee
Sonam Zangpo
Taiwan Payul Dharma Center
Taklung Tsetul Rinpoche
Taklung Monastery
Tara Tulku
Tarling Monastery
Taru Tulku
Thimphu Monastery
Temzin Gyatso
Tepa Lama
Tharig Tulku
Thi Shen Rinpoche
Thinley Norbu
Thinley Tharchin
Thutob Gonpo
Thugsrey Rinpoche
Thupten Dorjidrak Aewam Chokgar
Thuche Rinpoche
Thrulzhig Rinpoche
Thupten Choejor
Tibetan Mahayana Buddhist Mon.
Tingkye Gonjang Tulku
Tinlay Rabjay
Tulku Topgyal
Trubtob Rinpoche
Tshechu Rinpoche
Tseten Tashi
Tulku Longpo
Tulku Thondup
Tulku Topgyal
Tulku Tsonye
Thuthob Monastery
Urgyen Tulku
Varanasi Mahabodhi Society
Varanasi Nyingma Society
Varanasi Central Institute
of Higher Tibetan Studies

Gelug Lamas and Monasteries

Dent. Inst. Higher Tibetan Studies
Dechen Choephel Ling
Dharamsala Clinic
Drepung Lachi Monastery
Drepung: Loling Datsang
Drepung: Gomang Datsang
Dzongkar Chode Dratsang
Gaden Chhopelling Monastery
Gaden Choling
Gaden Jam Ghon
Gaden Jangtse Thosam Norling
Gaden Shartse Norling College
Gaden Tharpa Choling Monastery
Gaden Trijang Rinpoche
Gaden Tubten Choeling
Gaden: Jangtse Datsang
Gaden: Jangtse Datsang
Gelugpa Students Welf. Comm.
Ghadong Oracle
Gomang Wontrul
Gyudmed Tantric University
Gyuto Tantric University
H. H. Dalai Lama
H. H. Yongzin Ling Rinpoche
Kunsangling Nagtong Gonpa
LTWA
Nyanang Phelgyeling Gonpa
Palden Tashi Gomang
Samten Chholing Monastery
Sera Mahayana Monastic Univ.
Sera Mahayana Philosophy Univ.
Sera Thekchenling Lachi
Shelkar Chosde Gaden Legshad
Tamang Buddhist Association
Tara Tulku/Jimba Tulku
Tharpa Chholing Monastery
Theckling Monastery
Tibetan Youth Congress

Kagyud Lamas and Monasteries

Akong Rinpoche
Amchee Yonthen
Baro Kagyu Foundation Mon.
Bero Tulku
Choegyal Tulku
Chogyam Trungpa Rinpoche
Chokyi Nyima Rinpoche
D. Ontul Rinpoche
Dazang Tulku
Derge Khamtul
Dorzong Tulku
H. H. Gyalwa Karmapa
H. H. Gyalwang Drugchen
Kagyud Student Committee
Kanjur Rinpoche
Khenpo Ngedrub
Lama Wangdor
Tulku Pema Wangyal
Thrangu Tulku

Sakya Lamas and Monasteries

Bir Sakya Lamas School
Deshung Rinpoche
Gonna Rinpoche
H. H. Sakya Trizin
Jamyang Palden
Khenpo Appey
Khenpo Sangye Tenzin
Sakya College
Sakya Gompa
Sakya Monastery
Sakya Students Union
Sakya Thubten Namgyal Ling

PART SEVEN

Faces of

Refugees of Tibet

Young and old, women and men, in India and neighboring lands, the faces of the Tibetan people tell their own story, bridging past, present, and future.

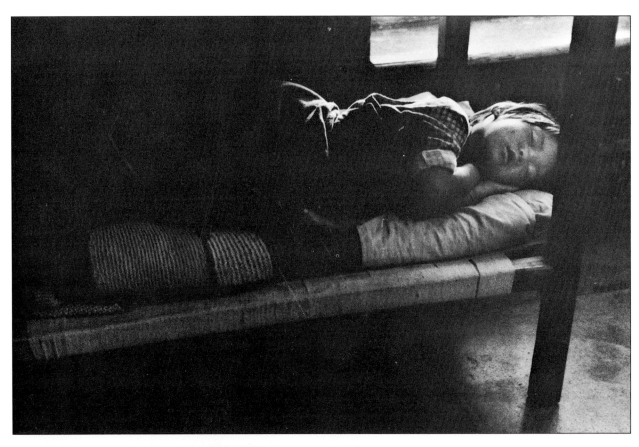

258

260

261

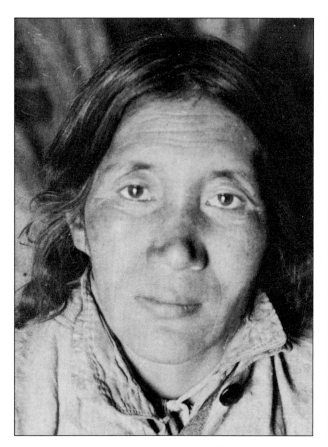

266

271

Cultural and Historical

Sites in Tibet

The maps on the following pages record some of the historic and holy sites in Tibet. Though exact locations and spellings are still being investigated, these preliminary research maps offer a glimpse of the ancient civilization of the Tibetan people. Many of these holy places date back to the times of the Dharma Kings in the seventh, eighth, and ninth centuries; other locations are birthplaces of important master or sites where gTer-ma were located; some are monasteries founded in early times.

Many place names are being added as research continues, and we hope to publish more complete maps in the future. Maps include some but not all of the regions of traditional Tibetan civilization, together with surrounding areas. No political boundaries are indicated or intended. The maps are at various scales and have some areas of incomplete relief. They are based on DMAAC maps, ONC Series.

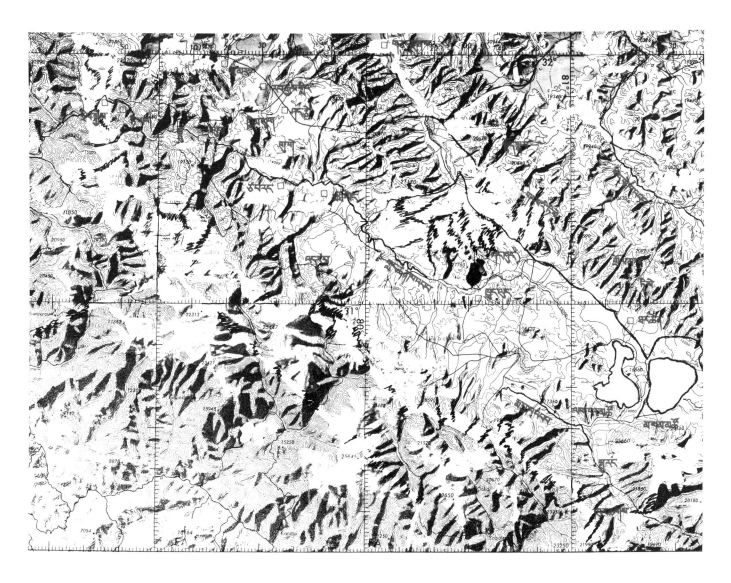

PARTS OF MNGA'-RIS

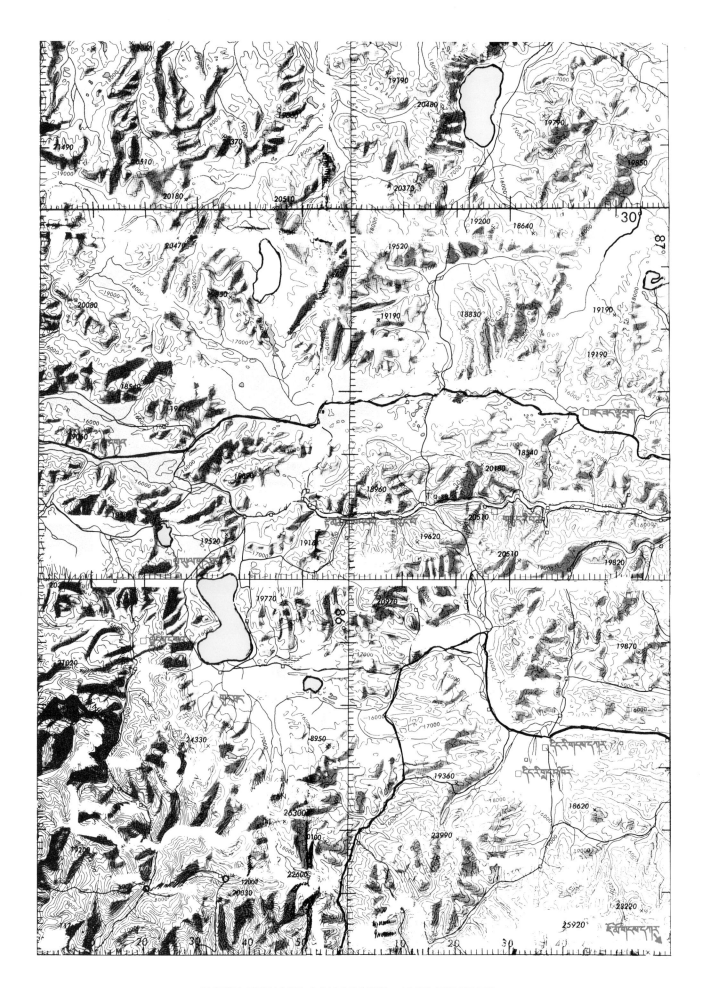

WEST GTSANG, MANG-YUL, AND DING-RI

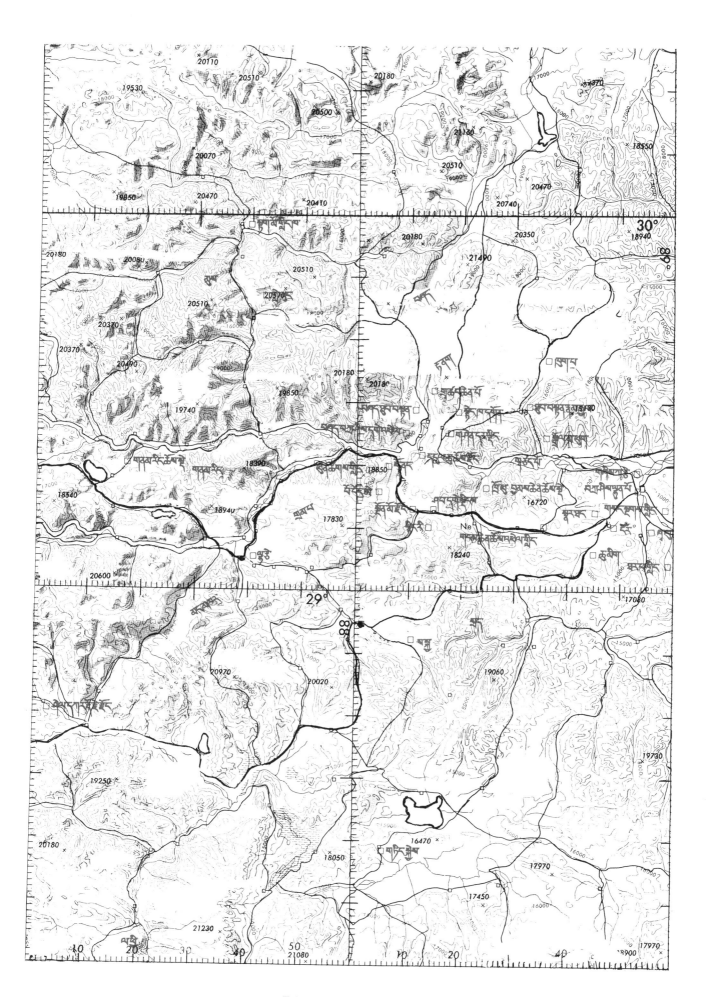

PARTS OF GTSANG

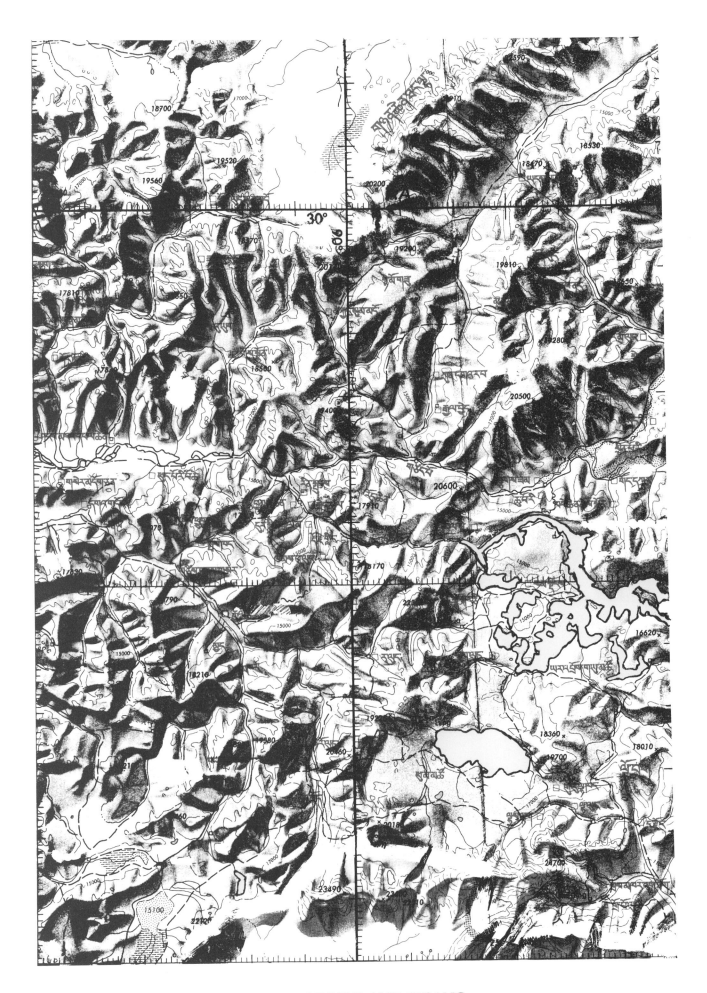

PARTS OF DBUS AND GTSANG

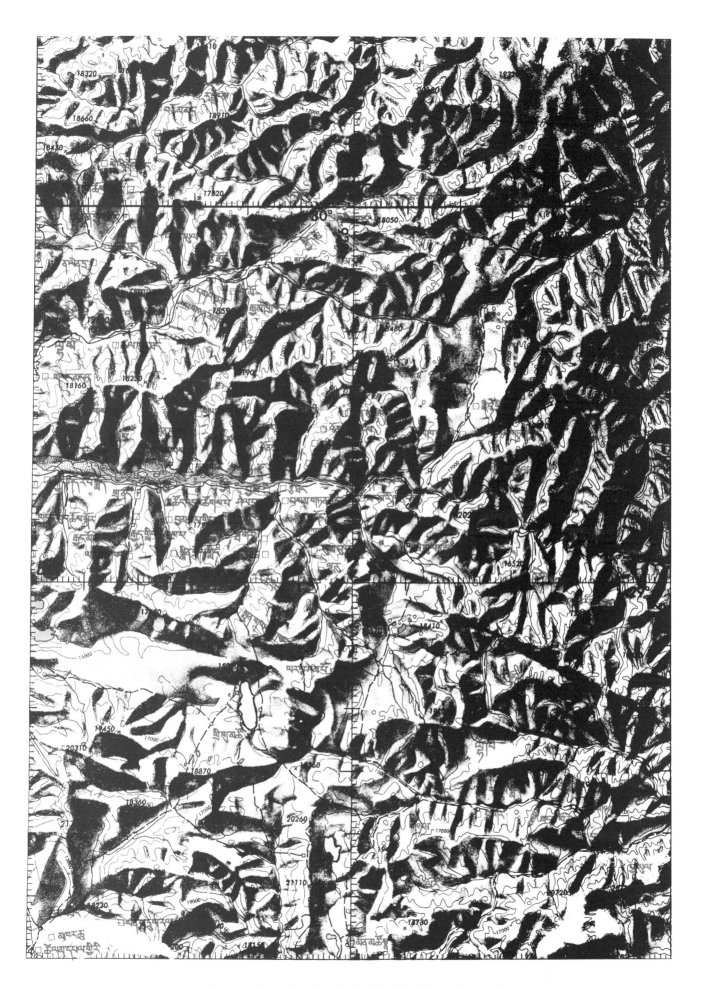

PARTS OF DBUS, KONG-PO, DWAGS-PO, AND LHO-KHA

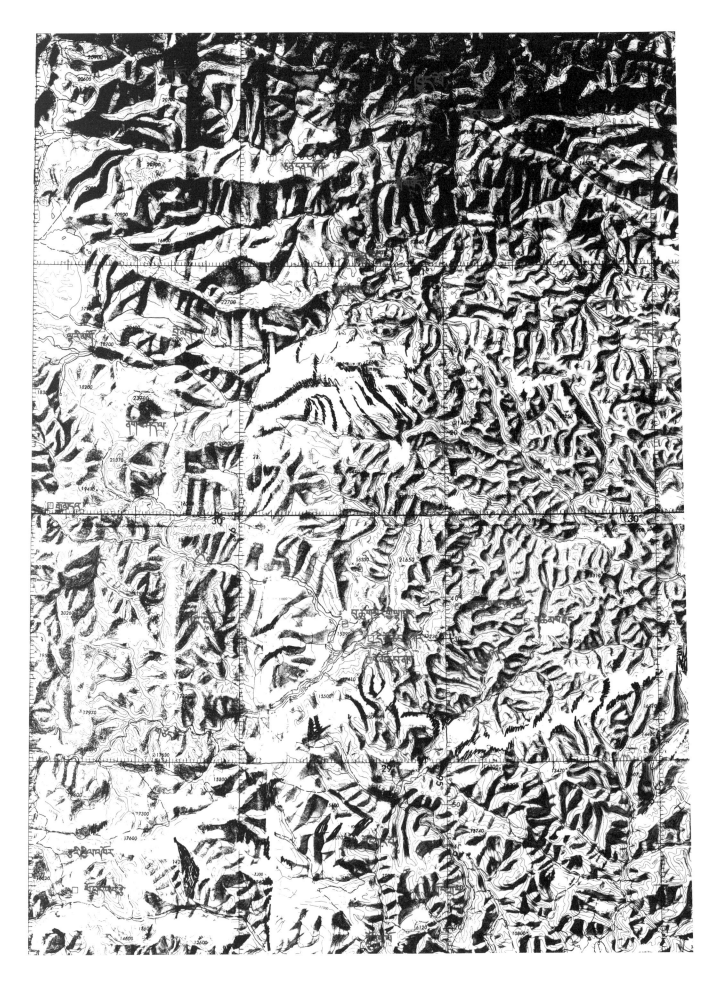

PARTS OF KONG-PO, SPO-BO, AND KHYUNG-PO

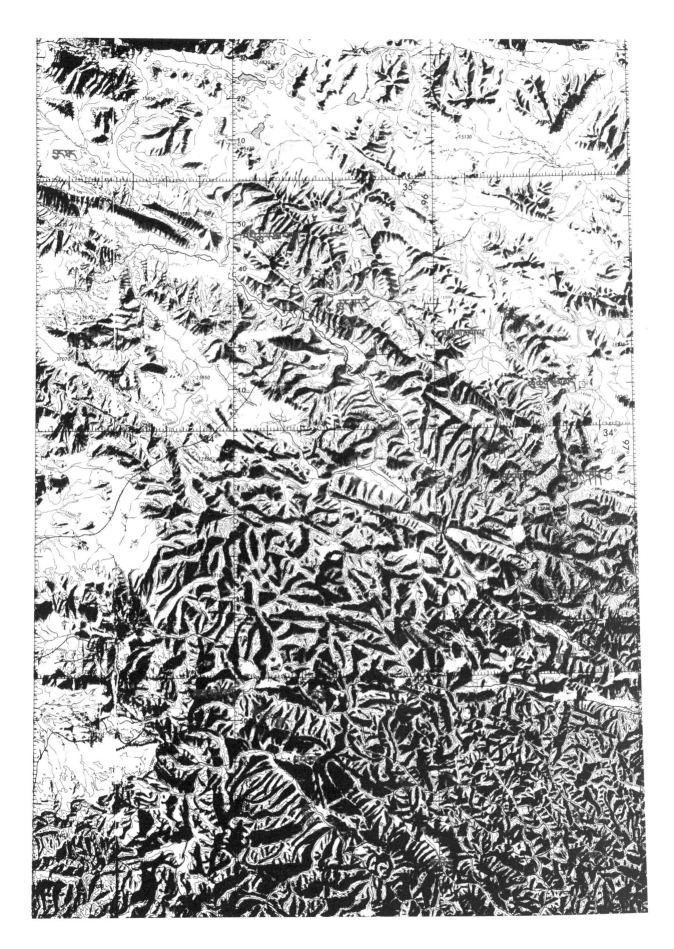

PARTS OF NANG-CHEN, SGA, AND BYANG-THANG

PARTS OF KHAMS

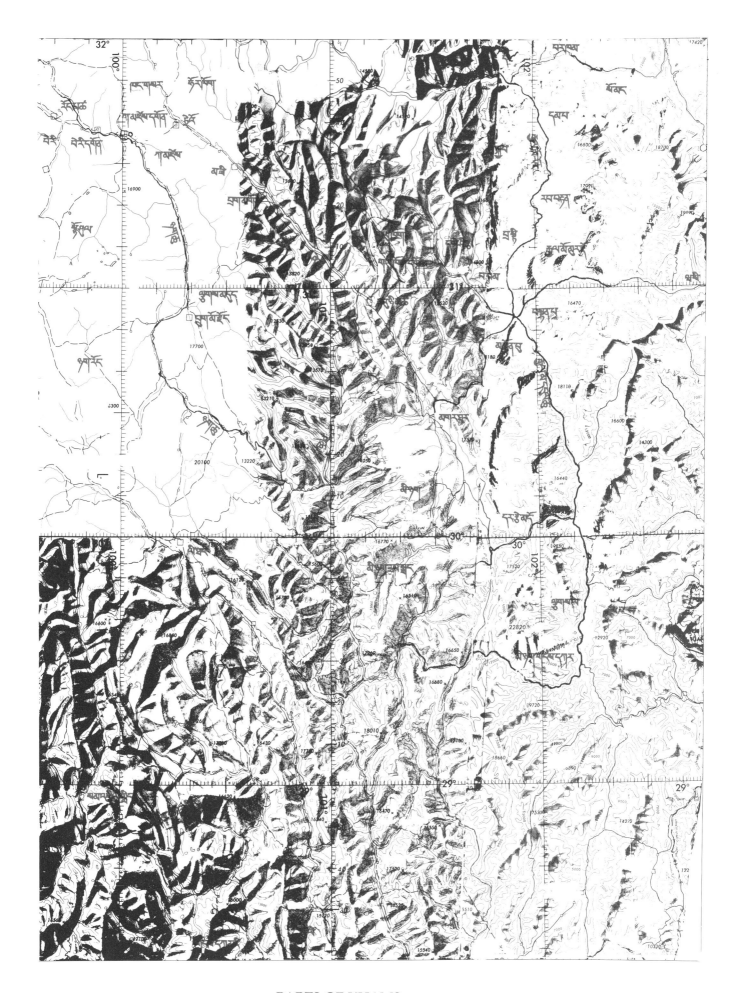

PARTS OF KHAMS

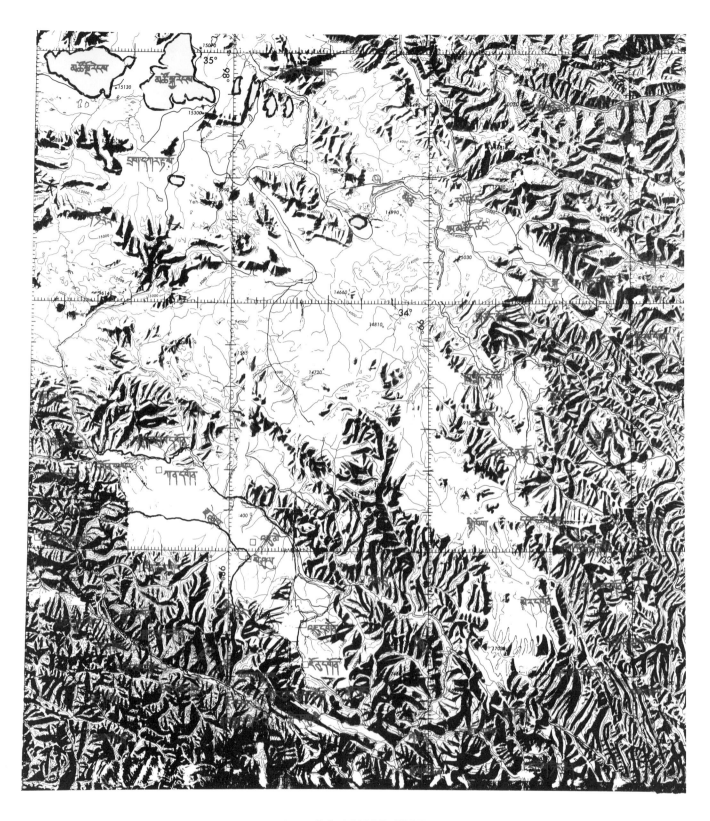

PARTS OF 'GU-LOG, NANG-CHEN, AND SGA

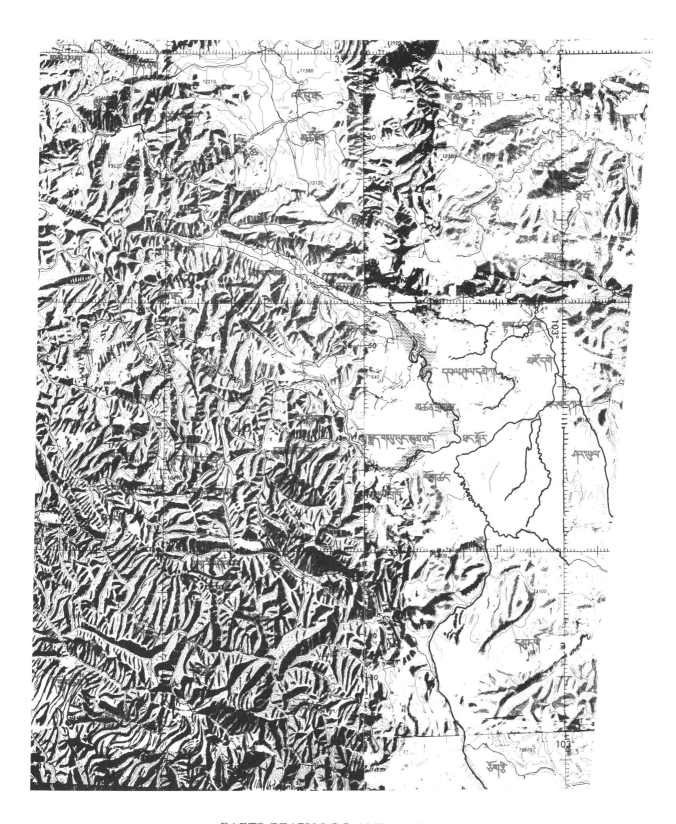

PARTS OF 'GU-LOG AND A-MDO

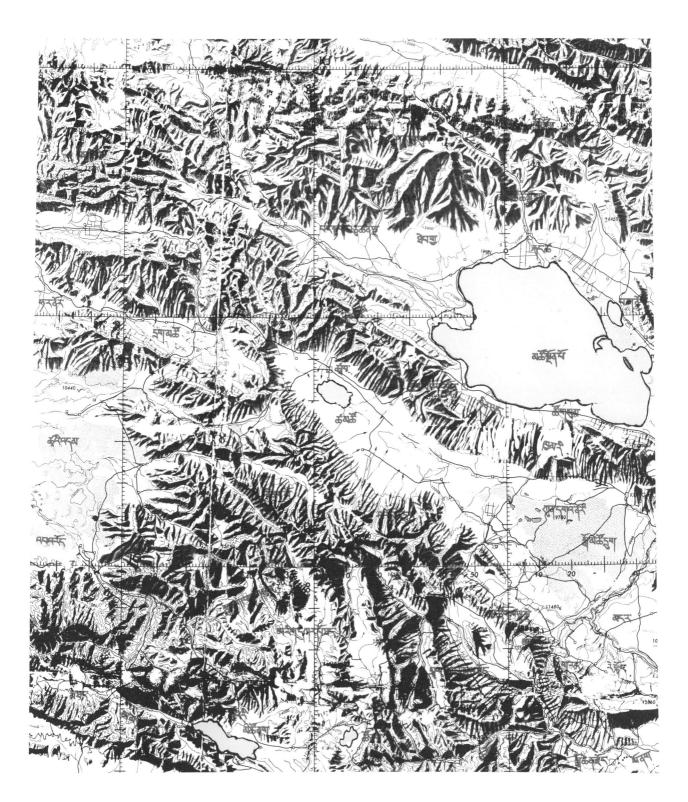

PARTS OF A-MDO

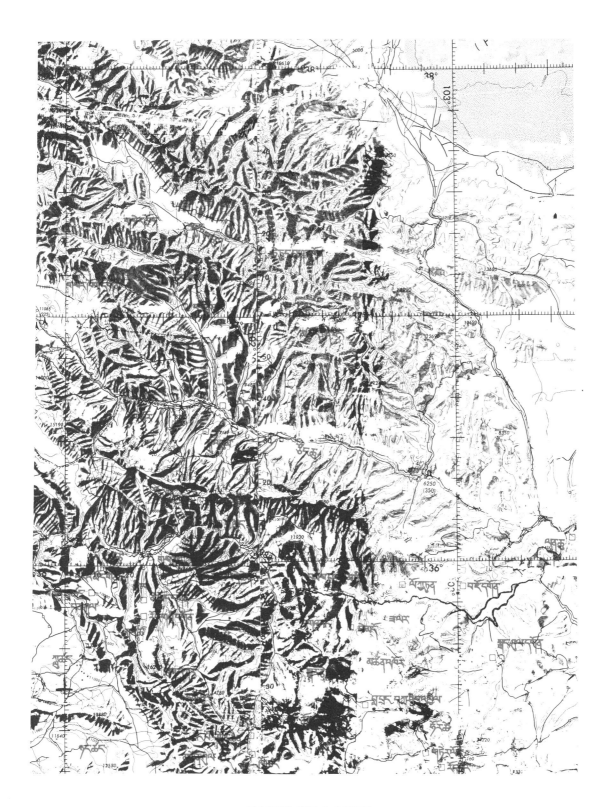

PARTS OF A-MDO

Historic and Holy Sites

ཤུད་པོ་རི་བོ་ཆེ	ཡུལ་བ་བྲག་སྐྱང	མོན་སྒྲུབ་སྒོ	ཅུར་ཕུ	བདྲག་ཕྱིས་བཞི་བ
ཁྲམས་པ་སྐྱིན	གཡའ་མ་ལྷ་ཁང	ཐྲ་ཀྲུང	འཕྲི་གུང	རྣོར་བྲིང
ཐྲ་ལམ་རྩེ	ཤར་ཚབ་གཞུང	རྒྱལ་མོ་རོང་དགོ་རྫོ	གདན་ས་མཆིལ	རྗོང་ར
རས་པ་ཕུ་ལ་སྐུར	ལྷོ་བྲག་ལ་ཁྲ་ཚ	འཕྱིང་རྒྱས་པར་བོ་དཀྱིལ	དགའ་ས་སྒྲ་སྣར་པོ	ཟར་ར་རི་ཁྲ་དཀར
རྫིག་གདགོན	ས་མ་ལཻར་དགོ་ཐོག	ཐྲ་ག་དཀར་བ་ཕྲིན་བཟང	བ་ལ་སྐྱུར་མ	གདར་རི་རོང་དཀར
ད་ས་པོ་རི	གཙང་བ་སྐྱ་ལ	རྒྱལ་མོ་རི་རོང་སྐྲ་ས་རྗེ་ཅིན	རི་བོ་ཆེ	གཉས་ནན
ཀྲི་སྒྱང	རི་བོ་དགའ་བཟང	ཡུལ་ས་ཟམ་རི་བོ་ཆེ	གས་ར་རྒྱག་མཆོ་མ་སྟྲོང	
མ་ཆི་ལམ་ཕུ	ཁ་འདུག	རྒྱ་མཚོ་ར་བ་རྩ་གསུམ	ཡ་ར་དགོན	
བསམ་ལ་ཡས	གཏོ་ཊི་སྒྲོ	སྐུ་རྗེ་ག་སྒྱ་བ	ས་སྐྱ	སྟོ་ལ་སྟྲང
སྒྲུ་སྒོ	ཅུ་རི	གྲོ་ལ་ག་སྒྱ་བ	རོ་ལྨ་ཁ་མཆོ་ས་སྟང	ཅུང་ལ་སྟྲོང
མ་ཁོ་ལ་མཆིང	གོང་པོ་ཡུ་ཚ	བསམ་ལ་ཡས	སྐྱི་དགོ་སྐྱུ་ནྲ་བྲ་སྐྲེ	རྒྱུ་མིག
གྲོ་མ་བ་སྐྱུར	ལྷོ་བྲག་ལ་ཁྲ་ཚ	སྐྱིན་བྲོ་བ་སྒྲིང	རྗོང་ག་ས་ར	ཀུ་ལུ
ཕྲ་རོང	སྐྱུ་ར་ང	རི་རྗེ་ལྲག	ཀུ་ལུ	རྒྱ་བ་ཕྲོག་ཡར་བ་ཕྲོག
ཐྲ་མཚ་ལ	བོ་ལུ་ག	གཡ༔ཕྲོ་ག	སྐུ་ར་ཁར	འཕྲི་གུང
བྲག་ཡེ་ར་བ	འ་ཕྲོ་རི་སྐྱུ་ག་པོ	ད་ལ་ཕུ་ལ	དག་ན་སྐྱུ	ཚ་བ་ལ
སྐྲུག་ལ་པ་ར་སྟོང	མ་ར་ཕུ་ལ	རྗོ་ག་ས་ཅིན	འཕྲ་བ་སྒྱུ་ར་མ	ཐག་གོ་སྒྲུ
ཤི་ལ་བྲག	ཁ་ལམ་རི་བོ་ཆེ	ཞི་ཅིན	ཞ་ར	གཡའ་བ་བཟང
ཟུར་ག་བ་ར་རྗོ	སྐྲ་མ་པོ	རྗོ་སྒྱུག་ཅིན	བདྲག་ཕྱིས་སྟུན་པོ	རྒྱ་བྲོ་དྲ་བྲ་ཕུ་ལ
བོན་ཞུ་རྒྱག་མཆོ	ཟ་ར་བ་སྒྱུ་ག	ད་ལ་ཕུ་ལ་དྲ་ར	ཚ་བ་མ་རོ	སྐྱ་ག་ཕྲང
བྲ་ཕྱུ	མ་མཆོ་ཕ་རྒུ་སྒྲིང	ཕྱུ་ག་སྟྲང་དགོན	སྐྱུ་ར་བ་ལམ	སྟོ་ད་ལྲ་ག